THE SEVENTH
THAT I AM

TERRY CLARK

ISBN 979-8-89309-776-4 (Paperback)
ISBN 979-8-89309-777-1 (Digital)

Covenant Books
11661 Hwy 707
Murrells Inlet, SC 29576
www.covenantbooks.com

The seventh month has come and gone, and what is its significance? The Bible describes the Feast of the Lord in Leviticus 23. It starts with the Sabbath day at the beginning of the chapter, being the seventh day, and then the first month, fourteenth day of the month being Passover. For seven days, Unleavened Bread, and then the Feast of Weeks or Pentecost fifty days later. The first day of the seventh month is the Feast of Trumpets. The ninth day of the seventh month starts the Day of Atonement. The fifteenth day of the seventh month starts, and it goes on for seven days, the Feast of Tabernacles. The eighth day is the Last Great Day.

It has been understood by religions as follows:

The Passover started in Egypt with Moses and the firstborn dying, except those that had the blood of the lamb on the doorposts of their homes. In Christianity, it was picturing Christ being the Passover Lamb taking away the sins of the world. The days of Unleavened Bread symbolize coming out of Egypt or sin. Some look at the Red Sea as baptism and eating unleavened bread as putting Jesus or Christ in you. We will come back to that later. Now for the Feast of Weeks or Pentecost, it is as Moses receiving the Ten Commandments or Law in the Old Testament and the receiving of the Holy Spirit on the day of Pentecost in the New Testament.

There are seven feast days in all, which are written in detail in the Old Testament and are kept by Jesus, the disciples, and His followers in the New Testament. Some places to look are Mark 2:27; Acts 2:1; Luke 2:41; John 5:1; 1 Corinthians 5:8; John 7:37, 7:2, 4:45; Matthew 5:1; Mark 14:1. In religion, it means all have been fulfilled by Jesus except the seventh month or the Fall Holy Days. "Trumpets" symbolize the return of Christ at the end of the world. "Atonement" is the putting away of Satan, and the "Feast of Tabernacles" is the thousand-year rule of God's KINGDOM on earth or the millennium. "The Last Great Day" is when all the dead are resurrected and judged in the "Great White Throne Judgment." There are many that know nothing about these days. Knowing about the days and knowing what they mean and what they represent are two different things, which we will get into later.

There are many things to believe, and all beliefs are true to the ones that believe them. Many believe what is written down, but the truth is deeper than what is believed or read—much deeper. We will see this more as we go on.

In Galatians 4:24, Paul tells the story of Abraham about his two sons, being the two covenants, one from Mount Sinai (or) of bondage which is Agar. This Agar is Mount Sinai in Arabia and answers to Jerusalem what now is and is in bondage with her children, but Jerusalem, which is above, is free, which is the mother to us all. These verses are covered from Galatians 4:24 through 26. This is deep spiritual knowledge which takes a story and places it as now. In verse 26, the mother to us all as being above, which religions would call heaven as in the sky, but I will say more about that later. Now you must keep an open mind as we go on. You don't have to believe anything, but you can think for yourself.

An allegory is a story in which figures and actions are symbols of general truths. In Galatians 4:24, things there are an allegory. The Bible is a spiritual book of truth; Thy word is truth (John 17:17). Jesus—I will talk about his name later—said, "I am the way, truth, and life." I will also talk about the words "I am" later. You must worship God in spirit and in truth (John 4:24). I will also talk about God's name later. The truth shall set you free (John 8:32). Free from what? I will talk about that later.

In 1 Corinthians 1:17, Paul said, "For Christ sent me not to baptize but to preach the gospel not with wisdom of words lest the cross of Christ should be made of none effect."

> Who also hath made us able ministers of
> the New Testament not of the letter, but of the

spirit: for the letter killeth, but the spirit gives life.
(2 Corinthians 3:6)

Keep this in mind. Now you know that all scriptures are given by the inspiration of God (2 Timothy 3:1), and it requires your efforts, though; study and rightly divide the word of truth (2 Timothy 2:15). In 1 Thessalonians 5:21, it is written, "Prove all things. So using three things, witnesses; if it's in God's word, scriptures, divided rightly." It can be proven, which is not just limited by the Bible but can be by history or plain facts, and you have studied it and if you have been called, which I will talk about later. Then it's the truth. It will stand.

You can read in John 18:37, "To this end was I born and for this cause came I into the world, that I should bear witness unto the truth. Everyone that is of the truth hears my voice." It doesn't say that everyone that is a Christian or a Jew or Catholic or Hindu or any other religion hears his voice, only those that are of the truth.

What is religion? Where did it come from? Now in Latin, it's the word *religare* which means "to tie down, to hold back, to bind fast." Not a word for bringing together at all. What is interesting about the word *religion* is what it had come to mean over the centuries, and not the word itself. You know *re-* means "again," and *legion* is a military term meaning "large army unit." It was used by the Romans for their armies' divisions of twelve thousand troops. Before that, it was a demonic term for twelve thousand demons. In Mark 5:9, there was one that was possessed by demons being called Legion because they were many. In the English language, *y, i,* and *e* are interchangeable in many instances. The word *religion* can be re-legion. What a term to be used for worshipping God. You are really saying; again colonizing demonic forces. Why do we use the word at all?

Now we will look at some history of not only Christianity but all religions. This can be proven, and I have proven this for myself for my satisfaction at best. The pyramids were built in 10,500 BC, before Christianity, where there was a birth of a god, which is Isis and Horus.

Now around 2500 BC, you could still find the statues of Isis holding her baby, Horus, which became Mary holding Immanuel or Jesus, which are still images used today by the Catholic Church. In fact, the Catholic Church used plagiarism in all its worship. Sun worship or paganism is worldwide in all major religions because of the Catholic Church, and hardly anyone questions it.

The sun was worshipped before religion and for good reason. Our only means of food for the longest time only depended on what came out of the ground. It was later that killing animals became another means of survival, more than likely because of the winters, where plants were harder to find. The days got shorter in the winter, and the plants that didn't die became mystical, where they had special powers. They were brought into homes to somehow bless the homes. It was evergreens, holly, mistletoe, running cedar, and the like. It was almost like a rabbit foot for good luck, based on superstitions, and is where this all started from. Barn fires were built in a circle to represent the sun along with plants being made into a circle and placed on doors for good luck. Does this sound familiar to anything else you know of? Jeremiah 10:1–5 describes this.

Now the oldest circle before this was the zodiac, where different stars were showed at different seasons becoming the constellations of twelve compassing the movement of the earth through the universe in our solar system. This is where astrology originated. If the truth be known, all religions have their beginnings in astrology. Let's view the movement of the sun through the constellations, starting with Virgo. The sun would go to the crux or southern cross constellation. Then on December 21, the sun is in its lowest point in the sky. Then the sun would stay in its lowest point for three and a half days, and on December 25, the sun would start its upward turn into the northern hemisphere, making the days longer.

Now you may be asking yourself, what does this have to do with religion? I will go back to Egypt with Horus, which was born from Isis, who was a virgin, and had a virgin birth. He was adorned by three kings, accompanying a star in the east. He was a teacher by age twelve. He was baptized at age thirty by Anox when he started his ministry. He had twelve disciples he traveled with. He performed miracles, healing the sick, and walking on water. Names like the Light," "the Lamb of God," "Good Shepherd," etc. He was betrayed by Tifephon and crucified and upon the third day was raised from the dead. That's one god. You have Attis of Frigrea in Greece who in 1200 BC was born of the virgin Naner on December 25. He was crucified and, after three days, rose from the dead. Krishna in India about 900 BC, born of the virgin Devaki. There was a star in the east showing his coming. He performed miracles with his disciples and upon his death was resurrected.

Dionysus of Greece, 500 BC, the same story. Mithra of Persia around 1200 BC, born of a virgin on December 25, had disciples, did miracles, was dead for three days and was resurrected to life. He was also worshipped on Sunday. This is only some of the saviors. Here's a more complete list: Krishna of Hindustan; Buddha Shakya of India whose mother is Maya; Salivahana of Bermuda; Zulis or Zhule, also Osiris and Orus of Egypt; Odin of the Scandinavians; Crite of Chalden; Zoroaster and Mithra of Persia; Boal and Taut of Phoenicia; Indra of Tibet; Bali of Afghanistan; Jao of Nepal; Wittoba of the Bilingonese; Thammuz of Syria; Atys of Phrygia; Xamolyis of Thrace; Zoar of the Bonzes; Adad of Assyria; Dava Tat, Sammonocadam of Siam; Alcides of Thebes; Mikado of the Sintoos; Beddru of Japan; Henus or Eros and Bremrillan of the Druids; Thor, son of Odin of the Gauls; Cadmus of Greece; Hil and Feta of the Mandaites; Gentaut and Quexalcole of Mexico Monarch of the Sibyls; Ischy of the island of Formosa; Xaca divine teacher of Plato; Fohi and Tien of China; Adonis, son of the virgin Myrra of Greece; Ixion and Quirinus of Rome; Prometheus of Caucasus; and last but not least, Jesus Christ, born from the virgin Mary in Bethlehem, which means the city of bread.

The wise men followed a star to a stable, and by the age of twelve, he was teaching in the temple. He had twelve disciples which followed him. He was baptized by age thirty and was crucified and rose from the dead after three days. Now this is where astrology comes into the picture. The constellation Virgo means virgin, and looking at the sign, it shows a woman (virgin) holding some wheat in her hand. It's like a "M" for Virgo, that's why Mary, along with many virgin mothers, start with the letter "M" as Myrra, mother of Adonis, or Maya, mother of Buddha.

Now Sirius is the brightest star in the east, which on December 24 lines up with the three brightest stars in Orion Belt, which are called then as they are also called now, "the three kings." As with the story of Christmas, the three kings always follow the star in the east to find the birth of the Son (sun), Jesus. You see, it's the same story in all these cases, with all these gods. In the mythology of the universe, Aquarius was the man, which was ruled by Uranus which was the god of heaven or by Saturn, that represents darkness. Saturn had another name called Cronus or time. Now Gaia, that's Mother Earth, gave birth to Uranus which was God. Just as Mary was conceived of the Holy Spirit (which was God) and gave birth to Jesus, which also was God. Now Joseph was the stepdad. Now Isis lay on Osiris's chest and was conceived by spirit and gave birth to Horus, and Osiris was the stepdad. Now Devaki was also conceived by the holy spirit and gave birth to Krishna, and Vasudeva was the stepdad.

So in all these cases, God is both husband and son which started with Gaia, Mother Earth, being impregnated by God to give birth to Uranus which is also God. Now Uranus is coming back in the Aquarius age, in the eastern skies, to reclaim his bride, or his children from Saturn, or Satan (another name for Saturn). We will talk more about this later in more detail.

The truth of all would destroy any one religion. This you can prove absolutely. It is just facts. You can look all this up in any library or on the Internet. Why destroy or discredit it? They are all trying to tell us something, if not the same thing, important. It seems to me to be the same thing. The truth shall set you free (John 8:32). We've been over this. It's not religion that sets you free. It is the way we are with religion that blinds us more than frees us. It's mostly lies that we've told so much, that we accept as truth, and really we haven't proven anything. In fact, any knowledge taken from a secondary source can't be trusted, even what I'm telling you. This is the kicker: most knowledge is taken from a secondary source. Anything can be written down or told. So how can you believe or trust anything that you don't know? Interesting, but what I've told you is, at best, documented and from various sources. Now let me share with you what can't be documented but I feel strongly is more than likely true.

Look at the word *good*. Now man has been around for some time now. It would stand to reason that he didn't learn everything at once. For thousands of years, survival was his only purpose. Like food and shelter and keeping warm. Now you are hunting, and lo and behold, there is someone else that is hunting in your area. Now they are taking away your means of livelihood; whether they know it or not, they are messing with your food supply. At first, you run them off, but they come back with more people and with weapons. This time they don't run off. Do you fight and get killed? Or do you kill them and in return get more people and even more weapons? I think most did this and who knows for how long? They made fences, then walls to castles and fortresses, and we still do. Only now, we're more civilized doing this. We think.

For survival purposes along with others, that someone must have said, "Hey, you know, it might be better not to die but to try to live." So communication must have been a problem at first, seeing there was no need for it except in your own family or clan. So gifts or peace offerings started, which is basically where trade comes from. So *good* became a means of survival. You traded with gifts being and showing good to others that were hunting the same things you were so you could live. They couldn't understand you, but they could see your kindness and they could see and receive the gifts. So good became equal with live, so to speak. It meant not being good wouldn't be equal to live, that it would be opposite, except they didn't know what opposite meant. They did know what backward meant. In this case, it meant not living was evil. It's funny that the word *live* spelled backward spells *evil*. I personally don't think this just happened by chance.

As families became groups, and then groups became clans, and clans became towns, and towns then became cities and communities, then states and countries, something happened. The gifts weren't big enough to give no matter how big they were. War was inevitable, by our own nature. It's necessary to have rules to govern people. We don't want to be told what to do, and everyone can't be right. Yet no one will admit they're wrong. So how do you control people that don't listen? Making them do good doesn't work. What is good for one, may not be good for another. Who determines what's good anyway? A control had to be made to govern people with less violence in which people wouldn't know they were being controlled. An invisible source of control or power that everyone would somehow agree on, but yet would not directly come from anyone. It would have to have rewards for being good and punishment for not being good, with guilt, superstition, and fear. That's how religion got into our lives.

Talking about lives, remember that *live* written backward is evil. We needed someone over the evil so no one would have to take all the blame so somehow we would be off the hook, in a way of speaking. Putting a D in front of the word *evil,* you have *devil,* and we have had him ever since. Now the word *good,* you take away one of the O, and you have the word *God.* Now depending on where you live would be which god you had. Not that this would take away wars, but it would make it possible to have some control over war. It would be caused by religions, and wealth could be made in the process. Millions would die by control over the masses, which is why the Catholic Church has Mass. It's also where the word *massacre* comes from, being that more people have been killed by the Roman Catholic Church than even war.

It's not that I'm putting down Catholics no more than I'm putting down any religion. It's some if not all religions that do this. If we'll just take an honest look at history, the world, and our own human nature, the truth about this is pretty plain. You would think that we would have learned this over thousands of years, but we haven't learned a thing. The Reformation, which brought on the dark ages, it was so bad to escape from this. We came to the new world at that time to have our religious freedom. So we could kill over seventy million Indians in the name of God.

Now you're not gonna find that in the history books nor are we going to find this information too easily. There are many that would go to great lengths to hide this information.

In Revelation 12:9, Satan had deceived the whole world. That includes religion. It also includes education, government.

We wrestle not against flesh and blood but
principalities. (Ephesians 6:12)

———

Rulers of darkness in high places—I will say more about Satan later. The world doesn't know it has been lied to by religions, education, and government because if it would have, it wouldn't have been deceived. We have talked about some history and facts about religions. Most religious people know nothing about this, and what I have talked about so far is not the half of it.

I will talk about control. It's easier to control people by what they believe and what they think, which would be by what they are taught to know than by force. That is why education is through the government and not the family like it used to be. You have homeschooling, but it's still regulated by state and government. We are told what to think and know and even believe, so we wouldn't really have to be regulated. That's how brainwashed we are. If you were just to look at history, we know the earth is round. Now why? About the year 1514, with Copernicus, the globe model was introduced, yet the fastest thing on earth at that time was a horse. Ships were wooden and stayed out of cold areas where ice would damage the hull or disable the ship. Balloons were not invented until 1760, and for twenty generations, we were taught the earth was round without any proof whatsoever, which shows that we only know what we've been taught. Part of this was due to the need for exploration. Trade by sea was the most prosperous for the fact of more goods at a time.

Most, if not all, taught the world was flat and that they would fall off if they went out too far. Now am I claiming to be a flat earther? No, I'm not claiming anything but facts. Richard E. Byrd, a great explorer, led an expedition called "Operation High Jump" in 1933–35 with 4,700 men to the South Pole. From that expedition, Richard Byrd came on a TV show called *Longines Chronoscope*. He reported that beyond the South Pole, a landmass as large as the United States, energy rich in natural resources, seven other countries were involved in the expedition. In 1955–56, there was another expedition led by Richard Byrd called *Operation Deep Freeze*; afterward, all missions stopped, treaties were signed, making the South Pole off-limits to all countries and people. This is the Antarctic Treaty System in effect by 1961. Now why? Now we may never know if we wait to be told. Why? What does the Bible say about this? Well, the flat earth thing anyway.

In Genesis 1:1, in the beginning, God created the heaven and the earth. It doesn't say it started with the universe with a big bang. In verse 6, it goes on to say, "Let there be a firmament in the midst of the waters, and let it divide the waters from the waters"; in verse 8, "He called the firmament heaven"; in verse 9, "Let the waters under heaven be gathered together unto one place, and let the dry land appear; and it was so." In verse 10, "God called the dry land earth, and the waters were called seas, and it was good."

Now if you look up *firmament* in *Strong's Concordance* (H7549), it means a visible arch or dome. Now let's confirm this in other places in the Bible. Psalm 18:9: "He bowed the heavens"; also 2 Samuel 22:10, "He bowed the heavens."

Now in *Strong's* (H5186), *bowed* means bend. Now to show this bent arch or dome is more than just space. In Isaiah 24:18, it said the windows of heaven are opened, and in Isaiah 13:13, God said, "I will make the heaven tremble." This firmament would seem to have substance, in order to tremble or to be compared to a window. The earth in Job 9:6 has pillars, and they tremble. In Psalm 75:3, it says "I bear up the pillars of it (earth)." In 1 Samuel 2:8, for the pillars of the earth are the Lord's, and he hath set the world upon them. In Job 38:4 and Isaiah 48:13, God laid the foundations of the earth and spanned the heavens. Now in *Strong's* (H2946), *spanned* means "to flatten out or extend out as a tent."

I guess the best description that can be given on this is from God Himself. In Isaiah 66:1, "The heaven is my throne and the earth is my footstool." This is also in Matthew 5:35 and Acts 7:49. What does a footstool look like? The legs would be as the pillars holding up the circle of the earth as Isaiah 40:22 describes.

What is interesting, Isaiah didn't say *ball*, like it is written in Isaiah 22:18 (toss thee like a ball). He knew the difference. There are many more scriptures in the Bible to support the flat earth theory. I haven't even started. I wanted to show you how deceived we are in knowing our governments, religious, and education systems. If this is true, why would this be hidden from us? Even our world on which we live. Control can be the only reason along with not giving up the power that you have. That's all I can come up with. They have to be the authority, and if they found the edge in 1961, and the world found out.

What else have they been lying to us about? The globe model would be a huge one. They would have to admit they don't know, and also that there's a God, who built this dome to protect us, and has been providing for us the whole time. That global warming, the space program, and the list goes on—it is all lies. Like I said, I'll come back to this later. Now back to religion and beliefs.

In Matthew 24:5, it's written, "Many shall come in my name and deceive many, saying I am Christ." Most say Jesus is Christ. There are many problems in that. One is that there was no *J* in the English language up until 1565, which means in the 1611 King James Bible, there was no *J* for *Jesus*. It was "Iesous." The Greeks' deity Dionysus was changed to Iesous, using *sus*. Now before that, it was Iesu, which was given to the new deity for Christianity by Constantine. The word *Iesu* meant passionless birth. Most prophets of old were called Iesu, being born from older parents. At the Council of Nicaea, Constantine declared that to be his name after the council could not come up with a name on their own. The new deity image was to be that of Serapis, which already had followers at that time called Christians. Christos or Christ were words being used long before Christianity.

The religion Mithra and all its doctrines were stolen by Nero when he destroyed all the temples of Mithra along with the Library of Alexandria in Egypt. Some of the doctrines and teachings of Mithra are as follows: heaven, hell, Sunday worship, a virgin birth, resurrection, repentance, grace, faith, tithing, and we didn't come up with these words or teachings on our own. In order for the Romans to have control by a world religion, they had to get rid of the others. It was as today with many different groups. The only main difference is that you got your head cut off if you didn't convert. If you were an Essene or a Mystic or had any Gnosis teachings, you were soon killed. Even today, Christians condemn the Gnosis, saying they are devil worshippers and not even looking into any of their teachings or facts.

What is an interesting thing is that *Gnosis* means knowledge. The *Gno* means to "know." You see it in the words *diagnosis* and *prog-*

nosis, and if you don't want knowledge, you can find it in the words *ignorant* or *ignore*. The Coptics weighed different truths with all beliefs and teachings and made a resolve. Like a policeman at a crime scene, we get the word *cop* from the word (*coptic*). The Christian religion also stole other teachings and doctrines from the Egyptians, Pagans, Hindu, and eastern customs as Buddha and Zoroaster. From the Egyptian god Horus, we get the word *horizon*, meaning "Horus rising" from the golden falcon flying east to west being Horus. Even the hands on the clock, the hour hand, being Horus, the minute hand being the moon, and the second hand coming from the second body in our solar system being Mercury.

Now baptism is a doctrine from Buddha for the water god "EA." When you break down the transliterations of that word, it comes to be known as John, and John the Baptist is the one to introduce baptism in the New Testament; before that, it's not found in the Bible.

Rapture is a strong doctrine of Christianity which is not even found in the Bible at all. Rapture is a Hindu teaching. You have Christian days which are religious holidays as Easter, Christmas, Halloween, which are nothing but carried over pagan holy days, where we get the word *holiday* from. The days of the week are named after the planets gods. Monday for the moon, Tuesday for Mars, Wednesday for Mercury, and Thursday for Thor or Jupiter, Friday for Venus, and Saturday for Saturn, and you know Sunday for the sun.

In many ancient books, "Looeamong" was the angel or demon behind the name "Christ," so that is not even trusted when you deal with truth, being that Christianity, Christian, Christmas, and our Savior's name all come from the word *Christ*. What you call something doesn't change what you believe in. Having the knowledge of where it comes from would help you understand it better, and what's wrong with that? Most don't know where their beliefs come from. Osiris was murdered by his brother Seth, thrown in the Nile, put in the sky by the god Horus, which is the constellation we call "the Great Bear." Isis, Osiris's wife, retrieved and revived Osiris long enough to have a child, which is a divine child she names Horus.

According to the myth, Seth tore the body of Osiris into fourteen pieces and scattered them across Egypt. This is represented by the annual cutting down and threshing of wheat and barley. Isis recovers all the parts except the phallus which is believed to be eaten by a fish. This is why thirteen is an unlucky number and is important in Mason and Halloween and many occult beliefs. This is where the obelisk comes from and words like *erect* and *erection*. Obelisks are found all over the world in churches and historical sites. It's where the Washington Monument comes from. Every church is built and set up according to this story.

The pulpit is called the head of the church, where the people sit is called the scrotum, and the steeple represents the phallus or male organ. The cross comes from the center of the zodiac clock, where the four spaces between the cross show the four seasons. Greek teachings were also put into the New Testament. Paul's letters, from the word *Paulos*, were actually from the travels of Apollonius of Rhodes. Most changes were made by the Roman Catholic Church. Does this mean not to believe anything in the New Testament? No, it just means to prove what you believe (see 1 Thessalonians 5:21).

On the side of a pillow in Egypt, older than any religion on the face of the whole earth, were the words (well, the pronunciation of the words) "Nok Pu Nok" and were not understood for over thirty-five years. I will tell you the translation of those words in a few, but for now, there are some other words I would like to look at. We freely say "God" and "Lord." We have talked about the word *God* along with the word *good*.

The fact of the matter is God and Lord are titles, not names. They have been used in place of Elohim and Yahweh. Elohim can be transliterated into "mighty one," Adonis from sovereign from Lord, and Yahweh from LORD with all capital letters. The true meaning of Yahweh was too holy to say by rabbis and priests, and the sentence of death was the law for many hundreds of years. The Jews hid the saying or pronunciation of the word by taking out the vowels so you couldn't say it. YHWH is what is written in many Bibles.

In Exodus 3:14, in the last part of the verse, "thus shall thou say unto the children of Israel, I AM, hath sent me unto you," Yahweh, pronounced in the Hebrew language "Yu-Hey-Wy-Hey," meaning I AM that I AM, happens to be the translation of the words at the beginning of this paragraph, "Nok Pu Nok."

The word *Hallelujah* has "Yah," in it which is God's name, I AM. In John 5:43, it's written, "I come in my father's name," and we have seen that Jesus is a Greek word, and there was no J until 1565. It also has nothing about the father in this name. Yahshua does and means "Yah saves." It's a Hebrew name, and another pronunciation is "Yahashavua." An important thing to remember is that names can't be translated where things can.

Things can be found in other places where you can call the same thing in another language. Names, however, are not the same in other languages. They must be transliterated correctly, hopefully with the correct meanings. Now the word *Christ* was used to replace the word *Messiah* or Chosen One. *Saviour* was also used. This has been taught and is so much ingrained in our thinking along with many teachings of Christianity.

There are many teachings in the Bible that religions are not going to teach or even address. For one thing, it would go against their religion and they wouldn't have a job. It's not a calendar on earth that has Sunday as the seventh day. It's always the first day of the week. It's easy to prove, most ministers even know it, but they will still keep and teach Sunday. Does it make a difference? Who would know? Everyone wants to hear the truth, but we won't be honest.

John 8:32 says the truth shall set you free. It's hard to believe the truth because to be honest, religion doesn't have any truth. No lie is of the truth (1 John 2:21). I will say again to keep an open mind. Once you hear something, you have the right to think for yourself. Religion, I have found, doesn't want you to think for yourself. Know this: there's truth in many statements, but if there is just one false thing in it, no matter how small, it makes the whole thing false.

It's like having a perfect meal with only a small amount of poison in it. Would you still eat it?

We have talked about allegories, which are spoken of in Galatians 4:24.

Jesus (Yahshua) spoke in allegory or parables all the time. In Matthew 13:10, His disciples came to him and asked him why he spoke in parables. In verse 13, it plainly said, "It is given unto you to know the mystery of the kingdom of God (Yahweh) and to them it is not given." Your mind, for one thing, must be opened. God (Yahweh) is no respecter of persons (see Romans 2:11; Acts 10:38; Colossians 3:25), but he doesn't give that which is holy to the dogs or pearls before swine (Matthew 7:6). For you see your calling that not many wise men, not many noble, are called. This is in 1 Corinthians 1:26. This is a chosen generation, a royal priesthood, a peculiar people (1 Peter 2:9). In fact, in John 6:44, "no man can come to Me except the Father which sent me draws Him."

You see, it is up to the Father (Yahweh) whether you can even come to Jesus (Yahshua) or not. Have you heard Christianity teach this? In Christianity, it's the Church's job to bring you to Christ. Not only that but to bring you into the Church. It makes itself the authority over your faith. Even though 2 Corinthians 1:24 said ministers and/or Church have not dominion over your faith, the Church's job is not even to save people or get members. Church means "a group, congregation or assembly" from 2564 in the *Strong's Concordance*. Only as the same true believers, *ekklesia* is its true meaning as being the called-out one. Its basis is on the word *Kaleo* meaning "to call, invite, or summon."

The authority of the speaker dictates the nature of the calling. In this case, the speaker is God (Yahweh). This is also translated to "name." To do something in someone's name is to do something in someone's calling or even way. We are talking about teachings, and the Bible teaches that which religions don't.

One teaching religion teaches us of heaven after one dies. Another is of God's (Yahweh) kingdom coming back and being set up on the earth. In Acts 2:29, it's written, "David is both dead and buried and his sepulchre is with us unto this day"; and in verse 34, "for David is not ascended into the heavens, but he said himself God (Yahweh) said unto my Master sit thou on my right hand until I make thy foes thy footstool."

I will talk about this right hand later and what that means. Another verse, John 3:13: "And no man hath ascended up to heaven but he that came down from heaven, even the son of man which is in heaven." The fact is we have not been taught the truth about death nor the truth of where we go when we die.

God (Yahweh or Elohim) said in Genesis 2:26, "Let us make man in our image after our likeness." Now we are physical and we think physical. So, therefore, we see God the way we are. In John 4:24, it said, "God is spirit and you must worship him in spirit and in truth." Now if you compare that with Numbers 23:19, which says, "God (Yahweh) is not a man." We can understand more about the Second Commandment, in which we should not make unto thee any graven images or any likeness of anything in heaven or in earth. Now the image or likeness talked about would stand to reason that it wouldn't be physical because God or (Yahweh) isn't. Let's look at what the Bible says about God or (Yahweh), who is spirit.

> Let God be true, but every man a liar. (Romans 3:4)

That is because Yahweh can't lie (see Hebrews 6:18 and Titus 1:2). God (Yahweh) is love, (John 4:8. What God (Yahweh) does shall be forever (Ecclesiastes 3:14). Keep this in mind: God (Yahweh) made everything by Yahshua or Jesus Christ (Ephesians 3:9; Colossians 1:16). Now in James 4:12, it's written, "There's one lawgiver to save or destroy." We have tried to make laws, but you see how the world is. In 1 John 3:9, it said, "God (Yahweh) can't sin."

First of all, what is that? Most religious people don't really know. In 1 John 3:4, it's written, "Sin is the transgression of the law, so sin is breaking the Ten Commandments."

"Now the wages of sin is death" (Romans 6:23). We have tried to keep the Ten Commandments; in fact, some churches have taught us to; others have just said they're done away with it. Yet Christ or (Yahshua) said, "If you would enter into life, keep the command-ments" (Matthew 19:17).

Now by Church teachings, sin has been taught to be anything from drinking to dancing, to sex, to not coming to church, to not tithing, to who you date or marry, to what type of job you have, to whom you go around or not around, on how you may raise your children, to what holidays or day you may or may not keep, to what you do, as smoking or cussing, or watching TV, the type of music you like or not like, on what you eat, as pork or seafood, to whether you would give blood or not. Yes, blood transfusions are a no-no in many religions.

The real kicker is this: you are not subject to the law of God (Yahweh) neither in deed can you be. That's Romans 8:7. The carnal mind (your natural mind) is enmity (hostility or enemy of) or better yet hates God's (Yahweh) laws and is not subject to them and neither indeed can be. That's what your Bible says. If you're in the flesh, and most people are, you cannot please God (Yahweh) (Romans 8:8).

Do you think joining a church or getting your head wet is gonna change this? What's the answer? In verse 9, "If you have not the spirit of Messiah (Jesus or Christ) in you, you are none of his."

The true image we have of God (Yahweh) is not physical.

> For we have not received the spirit of bond-
> age again to fear. (Romans 8:15–16)

What does that mean? We must have been slaves before, by saying again, and we must have been in fear also. Continuing with the verse: "But ye have received the spirit of adoption whereby we cry Abba, Father. The Spirit itself beareth witness with our spirit that we are the children of God (Yahweh)."

Our identity is made known to us by the Spirit. We also were slaves before by fear and guilt by religion. Hear me out. Fear and guilt were used to control us by religion and not only religion but everything that's physical. I will say more about sin later. One thing that is not told to us by the world nor religion is John 10:34:

> Then the Jews were going to stone Jesus (Yahshua). He said, "Many good works have I done of the Father; for which one of these do you stone me?" They said, "Not because of the good works but because you being a man maketh yourself God (Yahweh)." Jesus (Yahshua) said, "Is it not written in your law that ye (you) are gods?"

Read this in your Bibles. He wasn't talking to his disciples; he wasn't even talking to religious leaders of the day. He was talking to the Jews that wanted to kill him.

Another truth not known:

> There is no power but God (Yahweh). (Romans 13:1)

> There is none good but one. (Matthew 19:17)

Keep this in mind with Isaiah 45:7, which says, "I, the Lord, create good and evil." How can this be? This is one truth that's hard to swallow. If all power is but by God (Yahweh), then how this power is used is the factor that determines the outcome. If there is evil, it's only allowed by a greater power, good or God. Good and evil, light and darkness, in one sense, are all man-made concepts of the same power. Mistakes are made, but they can be corrected. Rights can be made wrong, and wrongs can be made right. Bad can be made good, and good can be made bad.

The devil and Satan control the evil and are used as deceptions by religious people mostly and even without them knowing it. No lie is of the truth (1 John 2:21). So any concept is as poison to a great meal if it's false. You wouldn't eat the meal if you knew it was poisoned. Yet people believe as truth what they have been taught, with no proof whatsoever.

Spiritual knowledge must be understood spiritually. There is truth in any language, but the first thing you need to understand is the language. Then the truth can be searched out.

> The letter killeth but the Spirit gives life. (2 Corinthians 3:6)

The Bible was written in ancient times. It has roots in mythology, mysticism, and even astronomy. We read in English things with different understandings, symbols, and concepts. It is a spiritual book.

> Therefore, leaving the principles of the doc-
> trine of Christ (Messiah), let us go on to perfec-
> tion. (Hebrews 6:1)

You mean you must leave doctrine to have perfection? Think about it. If you look at doctrine, you would be looking at physical things. Water baptism, you would be looking at water. Holy days, you're looking at days, Sabbath days, etc. Or laying on of hands, you would be looking at people. To understand this, you must consider symbols which were never used for worship. They represent other things, spiritual things, the ancients knew of (Psalm 78:2, Matthew 13) in parables. Then you have allegories spoken of by Paul in Galatians 4:24 and Proverbs 1:6 to understand a proverb or a dark saying. We use them every day, but years ago or even in the future, people wouldn't know what we were talking about. If someone kicks the bucket, we don't buy another bucket for the family, do we? If you're shooting the bull, do we really need a gun? If you spill the beans, who is responsible to pick them up? What's up? What's going down? It means the same thing.

A woman can be hot, a man can be cool or even a bad dude. You can plant yourself without going in the ground. This is all normal, and believe it or not, it sounds normal, but years ago, it would have been anything but normal. This is dark sayings. This is allegory, and this is parables that we know the meanings of. The Bible, being a spiritual book, is full of allegories, spiritual dark sayings, and proverbs. Don't you think it would be important to know its symbols?

In Genesis 2:8, God (Yahweh) planted a garden eastward in Eden with two trees. One was the tree of the knowledge of good and evil, and the other was the tree of life. You could take this literally, but I think you would miss the whole point. As the story goes, the serpent tempts Eve, and she eats from the wrong tree and gets her husband Adam to eat from the wrong tree also. After this, they are both kicked out of the garden of Eden, made to live in this world where they both would die.

The serpent, later to be known as Satan the devil, told Eve that she wouldn't surely die but would be as God, knowing good and evil.

Now religions have said that this was all a lie, yet in Genesis 3:22: "And God (Yahweh) said, 'Behold, the man is become as one of us, to know good and evil, and now, lest he put forth his hand and eat of the tree of life and live forever.'" Cherubims and a flaming sword, which turned every way to keep the way of the tree of life.

Now, remember, the garden was eastward. Keep this in mind.

> And on the east side toward the rising sun,
> shall they of the standard of the camp of Judah
> be. (Numbers 2:3)

If you look toward the north, the east is always on the right side. All through the Bible, the east and right side or right hand is used over and over again. Genesis 48:13–18, the right hand is used five times, showing the five senses. I'll talk about that later. Just in Psalms, the right hand is used over twelve different times (Psalm 16:8–11, 17:7, 48:10, 63:8, 73:23, 74:11, and "And the vineyard which thy right hand hath planted and the branch that thou madest strong for thyself" (Psalm 80:15).

Twelve is the number of perfection in Hebrew.

> Many pastors have destroyed my vineyard, they have trodden my portion underfoot, they have made my pleasant portion a desolate wilderness. (Jeremiah 12:10)

> Sit at my right hand until I make thine enemies thy footstool. (Psalm 110:1)

> Length of days is in her right hand. (Proverbs 3:16)

> A wise man's heart is at his right hand. (1 Kings 6:8)

In Solomon's temple, the door of the middle chamber was on the right side of the house, and they went up the winding stairs to the middle chamber and out of the middle into the third. In 2 Corinthians 12:2, it talks about this third: "I knew a man in Christ (Yahshua) above fourteen years ago (whether in the body, I cannot tell; God (Yahweh) knoweth), such a one caught up to the third heaven."

This sounds like an out-of-body experience; I will talk about this later. Now back to talking about the right hand.

Cast your net to the right side. (John 21:6)

When the Son of Man comes in his glory,
he will separate all nations as a shepherd divideth
his sheep from the goats, and he shall set the
sheep on his right hand, but the goats on his left.
(Matthew 26:33)

No wonder *right* is used as good, and also, *right* is used in the word *righteousness*; there's a reason.

Let's get up to date with where we are right now and what we've been over. The Sabbath, what it is, and what day? What is the Church and a calling? The true name of God (Yahweh) and his son (Yahshua)? The name Jesus, how it came about? How about death and heaven? Where is it? Yahweh not being a man? What is sin? About God's (Yahweh's) law? How about us and our nature? Being God or that there is no power but God (Yahweh)? How about a devil and the word *evil*? Spiritual knowing, given only by spirit? What is allegory and parables?

Which brings us up to this allegory of the right side or east that we have seen all through the Bible. We will be back to this right side and east, so keep this in mind, but in order to understand what the right side and east mean in allegory, you must look at the true teachings of Yahshua and what some have called the gospel of Jesus Christ. Now this *of* means belonging to. This was Jesus's (Yahshua) gospel that belonged to him, not a gospel about him but what he taught. It means good news in Greek and from a winner of a battle celebration in the original meaning.

Now in Mark 1:14–15, "Jesus (Yahshua) came into Galilee preaching the gospel of the kingdom of God, saying the time is at hand," which means the time is now. We will talk about this soon. Then you go to Luke 17:20, "When he was demanded of the Pharisees when the kingdom of God should come, he answered them and said, 'The kingdom of God cometh not with observation, neither shall they say, lo here or lo there, for behold, the kingdom of God is within you.'"

So, for one thing, you don't see it. Some are waiting to die to go to heaven, others are waiting for the kingdom to come. Now it is inside you, what does that mean?

> Woe unto you lawyers, for you have taken away the key of knowledge, ye enter not in your-selves, and them that were entering in you hin-dered. (Luke 11:52)

These verses no one teaches nor even talks about. So knowing the kingdom is in you, what does Jesus (Yahshua) or the Bible tell you first to do? Is it to join a church or get baptized or give your heart to the Lord?

> But seek ye first the kingdom of God and his righteousness, and all these things shall be added unto you. (Matthew 6:33)

Now remember, the kingdom is in you. Now go to Matthew 6:22: "The light of the body is the eye. If your eye be single, your whole body will be full of light, but if your eye be evil or double, your whole body will be full of darkness."

In 2 Corinthians 6:2: "Now is the day of salvation," just like Mark 1:15: "The time is at hand." Now in Luke 11:52, when it talks about entering in yourself, it is referring to meditation. It is also what is meant by if your eye is single. Seeking the kingdom first, since the kingdom is in you, is also entering yourself or meditation. Now this is allegory, and we'll learn more about if your eye is single.

In Genesis 32:30, when Jacob wrestled God (Yahweh), Jacob called the name of the place Peniel, for "I have seen God face-to-face." What is interesting about this, the pineal gland located between the eyes is known as the third eye. It is responsible for our dreams and is known for our connection with the divine. It is shaped as a pine cone and its symbol is the pine cone seen on the sides of driveways, stairways, staffs, and crowns on popes and kings the world over. This was the eye spoken of by Yahshua in Matthew 6:22.

Going in your closet in Matthew 6:6, which is allegory for going inside yourself. This is meditation. In Matthew 6:25–34, it is mentioned about taken no thought five times represented the five senses. The five senses are where all our knowledge comes from. In meditation, you take no thought, and you cut off any knowledge coming in these areas. It's touch, taste, sight, hearing, and smelling. This is written five times and is throughout the Bible. It's either showing the five senses or it's showing the five stages of consciousness. The five wounds Jesus (Yahshua) had on the cross show the five senses, the human element in overcoming in this life.

There are seven energy centers in your body taught by all the major religions of the world except the Western ones. Christians, Jews, Catholics were forbidden to have this knowledge. For one thing, if the kingdom of God (Yahweh) were in you, what would be the need of the church? They would lose their power and control. Through all the ages, this knowledge has been there. Yet men love darkness more than light.

> Hear another parable: There was a certain householder which planted a vineyard and hedged it roundabout and dug a wine press in it and built a tower and let it out to husbandmen and went into a far country. And when the time of the fruit drew near, he sent his servants to the husbandmen that they might receive the fruits of it. And the husbandmen took his servants and

beat one, and killed another, and stoned another. Again he sent other servants more than the first, and they did unto them likewise. But last of all he sent his son, saying, 'They will reverence my son.' But when the husbandmen saw the son, they said among themselves, "This is the heir; come, let us kill him and let us seize on his inheritance." And they caught him and cast him out of the vineyard and slew him. When the lord therefore of the vineyard cometh, what will he do unto those husbandmen? (Matthew 21:33–40)

The history of Horus, Attis, Krishna, Mithra, Buddha, and Jesus or Yahshua, John, and you can go on and on. All had the same story: being born of a virgin. The vineyard is the mind, in fact, the right side. Your mind has two hemispheres. The garden of Eden was eastward or on the right side. Judah was put on the east, the rising of the sun, which had 186,400 people in it, that happens to be the speed of light. The vision of Isaiah in Isaiah 1:1: Ahaz and Hezekiah mean strength and wisdom, which come from the right side of the brain. In Psalm 80:15, the vineyard was planted by God (Yahweh) on the right side. In Jeremiah 12:10, the ministers, the righteous religious pastors, have destroyed the vineyard because they haven't taught this truth of meditation of the eye being single spoken of in Matthew 6:22.

In Solomon's temple, when it was put together and built, there was no sound. There were no hammers, axes, or tools of iron heard, and it was built of stone (1 Kings 6:7). Why no sound? That is because this is referring to meditation. The middle chamber is the pineal gland, the winding stairs refer to the spine. This describes the brain. The seven chakras or energy centers of the body go up the spine. Starting at the base of the spine, it reaches the pineal gland and opens up the right side of the brain. This is done through meditation.

The Muladhara chakra is known as the curled snake, curled three and a half times. It is the first chakra at the base. Its element is earth. That is ambition, power, base or basic instinct, or plain ego.

The second is Svadhisthana, which is in the sexual area, which means "her favorite resort." Its element is water. It is desire, lust, repressed sex, etc. The third is Manipura at the navel. It means the city of the shining jewel, its element is fire, which is self-centered. It's our way or the highway. It's where religion is today. No one has an opinion. These three chakras must be overcome to even have peace with oneself. Now no knowledge can change this unless you do what Jesus (Yahshua) says.

> Why call me Lord, Lord, and do not the things that I say? (Luke 6:46)

Meditation and the single eye in Matthew 6:22 and seeking first the kingdom of God (Yahweh; Matthew 6:33), that is in you (Luke 17:20. These three chakras are called the animal nature, and as an animal, it's very predictable. The fourth chakra is Anahata, the heart chakra. It means "not hit." It's the sound that you do not hear. It represents the human spirit, strong feeling, and caring, emotion, and compassion. The fifth chakra is Vishuddha, the throat chakra, representing truth. It is purification and clearness, it shows wisdom. The sixth chakra is Ajna, it's called "the white horse." It is the pineal gland. White being pure and horse, meaning wisdom together as "pure wisdom." We will talk about the white horse later on.

The last chakra, the seventh chakra, is Sahasrara, the crown chakra. Its element shows one thousand petals, which will be talked about later. Coming up the spine through the seven chakras or energy centers, by focusing on the center of your head between your two eyes, the energy reaches the pineal gland and then the crown chakra and opens up the right side of the mind, allowing spirit to flow through all the chakras and give life and insight throughout all the person being.

Now more insights into the chakras, starting with the Muladhara chakra, the curled serpent of three and a half times. The spine itself is shaped as a serpent, and the reason for it being curled three and a half times has great importance for our being and our purpose and our reason for being.

> And I will give power unto my two wit-
> nesses, and they shall prophesy a thousand two
> hundred and threescore days, clothed in sack-
> cloth. These are the two olive trees, and the two
> candlesticks standing before the God of the earth.
> (Revelation 11:3–4)

This goes along with Zechariah 4:11–14:

> Then answered I, and said unto him, "What
> are these two olive trees upon the right side of the
> candlestick and upon the left side thereof?" And
> I answered again, and said unto him, "What be
> these two olive branches which through the two
> golden pipes empty the golden oil out of them-
> selves?" And he answered me and said, "Knowest
> thou not what these be?" And I said, "No, my
> lord." Then said he, "These are the two anointed
> ones that stand by the Lord of the whole earth."

Now you may not yet see the connection of these verses and
the curled serpent and the three and a half, but I'm about to explain.
This is where the zodiac comes in. It is as a clock with twelve constellations, three decans for each. Being twelve times three equals
thirty-six, and you add a zero for the 360 degrees of the zodiac circle.
You then multiply 360 by three for the three curls of the snake, and
you have 1,080.

Now you still have a half to add of the curls of the serpent. Half
of 360 degrees is 180. Now you add 1,080 and 180, and you have
1,260, which would be 360 times three and a half equals 1,260. Now
this is the same number as in Revelation 11:3, which talks about the
two witnesses prophesying for one thousand two hundred sixty days,
and refers to the two olive trees and the two candlesticks which are the
pineal gland and the pituitary gland that produce claustrum which
flows through the spine. This may sound crazy now, but in Zechariah
4:11–14, it talks about it being on the right side of the candlesticks

and of it emptying itself with golden oil from two golden pipes. The right side being the right side or spiritual side of the brain. Being in allegory with deeper meanings than what is written.

Now what is interesting, if you look at each of these numbers and add each number together on out, you will always come out to nine. Not counting the zeros. Three hundred sixty as three plus six equals nine; 1,080 as one plus eight equals nine; and 180 as one plus eight equals nine; and 1,260 as one plus two plus six, which equals nine. That is because the number nine means consciousness. This is throughout the Bible. In Revelation 14:1, talking about the 144,000 it adds up to nine. One plus four plus four equals nine, also Revelation 7:4 about 144,000.

Now in Revelation 13:16–18, it talks about the mark of the beast being 666. That's six plus six plus six equals eighteen, and one plus eight equals nine. The Bible tells you this in Revelation 13:16–18, saying it is the number of a man. Now numbers and language go together. In Sanskrit, Hebrew, Greek, Roman, Latin, and English, the letter values are the same the number of a man. Adam was shown to be the first man and is where the word man is transliterated from. We have found that there was no J five hundred years ago. J and I have the same number value. So A is one, and B is two, and C is three, and D is four, and so on.

Adam would be A, I is one, and D is four, and A is one again, and M would be twelve. So one plus four plus one plus twelve would be eighteen, and one plus eight would be nine. Also, J and I happen to be the ninth number value. Now you take any number and multiply by nine, and then add the answer number together, and then that answer of those numbers together, and you are always going to end up with nine.

Some examples are the following: 7,942,751 times nine equals 71,484,759. Now seven plus one plus four plus eight plus four plus seven plus five plus nine equals forty-five, and four plus five equals nine. I will do one more, and it can be any number, like 5,331,179. Now multiply that by nine, it equals 47,980,611. Now add each number together, and you have thirty-six. Now add three and six, and you have nine. It's a very important number and has great spiritual truth throughout the Bible. It is also a number of creation. The earth is tilted 23.4 degrees, which adds up to nine. The precession of the equinoxes, which is twenty-five thousand nine hundred twenty years, adds up to eighteen, and one plus eight equals nine. Each constellation takes two thousand one hundred sixty years to get through, moving one degree per seventy-two years, each of these numbers adds up to nine.

Seventy-two is the average age, temperature, and pulse. There's a relationship to time as well. It's 1,440 minutes in a day; it adds up to nine. There are 86,400 seconds in a day; that adds up to nine; 10,080 seconds in a week, and 525,600 minutes in a year, all add up to nine. Music was pitched to 432 hertz, which added up to nine, and was changed to 440 for some unknown reason. It is as if to get people out of sync with nature. It is the number of consciousness. It takes nine months to be born. The beast in you is your lower consciousness, but the 144,000 that are saved are those that have the higher consciousness or God consciousness. Some say Christ consciousness. No thoughts mean no sin.

Remember in Romans 8:7, the carnal mind is not subject to the law of God (Yahweh), neither indeed can be. So you (yourself) can never change. That's why the virgin conceives. Virgin consciousness comes from no thoughts, which is the true Christ story, or son of Yahweh. Let's look at the Christmas story in allegory. We are the ones who are the shepherds that are watching the sheep or thoughts.

When someone has trouble sleeping, they are told to count sheep. Where did that come from? This goes back thousands of years.

> There is no new thing under the sun.
> (Ecclesiastes 1:9)

You can believe that. Now you are watching the sheep, and then come the wise men from the east. These are the new thoughts or enlightenment which come from the east or the right side of the brain, the emotional and spiritual or God (Yahweh) side of the brain. The wisdom from the right side and the shepherds go to the stable. The stable is us or the human body. The animals around are our physical nature. That's why there's no room at the inn. That is our physical nature or lower nature, our human nature, which is always too busy. It doesn't have time for God (Yahweh). The virgin or Mary is pure consciousness, and the star is the higher light which comes through the seventh chakra or the crown chakra. We go to the quiet stable of no thoughts, which is meditation, so the child can be born. This is what the world keeps as Christmas. The intercourse of the spirit to the Christ or virgin consciousness.

This is Christ in us, the hope of glory (Colossians 1:27). This is why marriage is holy and is the spiritual purpose of sex. This is the mystery, if you can receive it (Ephesians 5:32). It's allegory, the wise men, the star, the shepherds, the sheep, the stable, the birth of the child, the virgin. This story must happen within us. That is why in Acts 17:24, it is written that God (Yahweh) dwelleth not in temples made with hands. The only temple made in the universe without hands is on the sides of your head.

The allegories of the seven chakras are all throughout the Bible. Joshua 6:1–5: Seven priests shall bear before the ark seven trumpets of rams' horns and go around or march around the city one time a day for six days. Then on the seventh day, march around seven times that day, and with a long blast with a shout. The walls of the city shall fall down. This is the story of Jericho. The march around the city refers to meditation, that each chakra represents a circular energy center as going in a circle, as going around. Six days is six chakras, and the blowing of the trumpets we will talk about later, referring to the pineal gland. All six are done before the seventh, and then on the seventh, the walls come down.

This is the veil or divider between the right and left hemispheres of the brain, that the Spirit or God (Yahweh) can purge the left side. In John 2:1–10, it shows where the water was turned into wine. It was six waterpots of stone that were filled. In verse 8: "He said unto them, draw out now and bear unto the governor of the feast." And they bear it. The other six were filled to the brim.

In verse 7, more water was drawn out to fill the seventh pot, and when this was done, the water was made into wine. The six water pots had to be filled first. The allegory is the six chakras to be opened in order for the seventh to be opened. The wine represents Spirit, and it was at a wedding. In Matthew 22:1–14, the word *wedding* was written five times, showing the five senses which is us.

> The marriage of the Lamb is come, and his
> wife hath made herself ready. Meditation is the
> means of making herself ready. (Revelation 19:7)

Why is "her" used or wife used for church or follower of Christ (Yahshua)? It is because the right side is the emotional and spiritual side, which is feminine, and the left is the intellect or physical side, which is masculine.

> Watch ye, therefore, and pray always, that
> ye may be accounted worthy to escape all these
> things that shall come to pass and to stand before
> the Son of Man. (Luke 21:36)

In Mark 13:33–37, *watch* is written four times, showing the four attributes of man: physical, mental, emotional, and spiritual, which we purge by meditation; that is what watching is.

That is why it is watching and praying. Some have suggested it was looking at world events, but how would that, in the context of the verse, make you worthy to escape what's going on in the world and stand before the Son of Man? In Daniel 3:21, it's the story of the fiery furnace, where the three (Shadrach, Meshach, and Abednego) were thrown. There was a fourth formed in the fire like unto the Son of God. That is in verse 25. They heated up the furnace seven times more than it was to be heated in verse 19.

This is an allegory, showing meditation. It's the seven chakras being heated up. It is by the Spirit burning or purifying the other three attributes of man—physical, mental, emotional—that all four are saved. In Revelation 5:1, the book in the right hand of him that sat on the throne (the right hand is the right side of the brain). We have talked about in Genesis as Eden being eastward and Numbers 2:3 about Judah being placed on the east or right side toward the rising sun, which, looking toward the north, east is always on the right side. Jeremiah 12:10 and Psalm 80:14 refer to the vineyard being planted on the right side. In Matthew 25:31, the sheep are placed on the right side, and the goats on the left.

Now to finish the verse out because we are still in Revelation 5:1, that says the book that is in his right hand was written within and was also on the backside, sealed with seven seals. Look at within, and look at backside.

Within you (it is spiritual) and the backside is your spine. It is where the seven energy centers are, up and down your spine, the seven chakras. This also is the Book of Life. This is deep spiritual knowledge, and where does this all originate?

It's basic astrology. You can't understand the Bible if you don't understand astrology. The world and many religions would be offended by this. You also can't understand astrology if you don't understand the zodiac. You know spring cannot come until the last part of March into April, which is Aries the ram. Why a ram? This animal is used for sacrifices for centuries in many religions. Why?

The sun represents the fire that burns the sacrifice (the ram) before spring (the new life) can come. In most calendars, spring begins the new year. Why? This is why. New life. It's in the Bible, now it's hidden for most, but let's find it. In Romans 1:20, for the invisible things of him from the creation of the world are clearly seen, being understood by the things that are made.

Every year, spring comes (new life begins), which shows new life should begin in us. In the fall to the winter, things or life dies, showing that we are to die or become the sacrifice in order for Christ (or new life) to be born in us. It has been happening in the universe and on the earth forever. This plan and/or purpose of what is the real salvation is written all throughout the Bible in allegories, with the creation and the zodiac, that is in line with meditation and using the chakras.

In Genesis 22, the story of Abraham, when he was to offer Isaac up for a sacrifice, the allegory of this is he had to go to the place that he was told, which was up on a mountain, but when he got there, a ram was already there for him. The mountain allegory is going up the spine through the chakras in meditation where the sacrifice is made there for us, as Christ is at the Father's right hand. In Luke 22:10 and Mark 14:13, before Yahshua (Jesus) died or was sacrificed, two of his disciples were told to go into the city: "and there shall meet you a man bearing a pitcher of water, follow him."

Verse 15 of Mark 14 says, "And he will show you a large upper room (furnished) and prepared there and make ready for us." The man with the pitcher of water is Aquarius in allegory, which is the new age we're coming into.

The upper room is the right side of your mind that you go into in meditation using the chakras. The Manipura chakra or the solar plexus (why solar?) is represented as the sun or fire (the energy coming up the spine), the seven chakras to the pineal gland to burn up the sacrifice, which is Aries or ram or Christ or you. Then the new life begins. Yahshua (Jesus) in Revelation 3:14 calls himself the Amen, which refers to (Amun Ra) the sun god of Egypt. Why? Because Christ in you is the hope of glory (Colossians 1:27).

The solar plexus, the sun, the fire, the Spirit, meditation, the way. Virgo is the virgin that conceives the pure consciousness of no thoughts that Christ can be born. Krishna, chrism, was later changed to claustrum, a spinal fluid produced by the mind which becomes a golden substance in the pineal gland and a milky substance in the pituitary gland. This is what produces the mother's milk in the breasts of new mothers, which was the only source of life for thousands of years, the only food for newborn infants. Before any religions that we know of, this fluid was called Holy Claustrum, then later on it became Saint Claustrum, and then Santa Claus, coming down from the North Pole, giving life (gifts) to the children. As of recent times, the pineal gland along with the pituitary gland have been proven, when activated, to produce serotonin and melatonin, which have many health benefits from killing cancer cells to strengthening the immune system.

Now, in allegory, the land that flows with milk and honey, it's not talking about a land at all. It's talking about what the pituitary and pineal glands produce. In the book of Proverbs and the book of Solomon, honeycomb is used showing these two glands. Examples are Proverbs 19:10, 16:25, 21:7, 24:13. Now in the Songs of Solomon 4:11:

> Thy lips, O my bride, drop as the honey-
> comb: honey and milk are under thy tongue;
> and the smell of thy garments is like the smell of
> Lebanon.

In allegory, the lips are a part of the mouth used in speaking; in this case, it would be the bride speaking, which the Bible refers to in Revelation 19:7:

> The marriage of the Lamb is come, and his
> wife hath made herself ready.

So we are the bride. We speak through the Spirit by the honeycomb with milk and honey (which is the pituitary and pineal glands), and "milk and honey are under thy tongue" means that the narrow gate is used in meditation, where the tongue is placed in the roof of the mouth, giving a more direct route for the energy of the seven chakras coming up the spine to get to the pineal gland. That is located between the eyes, more toward the center of the brain. That area of the roof of the mouth under the pineal and pituitary gland is actually called the narrow gate spoken of by Christ (Jesus, Yahshua).

> Narrow is the gate and straight is the way
> that leads unto life and few be that find it.
> (Matthew 7:14)

The garments are to be white (Revelation 3:8), for they are worthy, and the prayers of the saints are as sweet incense (Revelation 5:8). They are pure and worthy. Lebanon in the Bible is known for its cedars, and the high hills and mountains are mentioned along with the valley and the river Euphrates. In allegory, it is a highly regarded place as being as the kingdom of God (Yahweh) that is within you (Luke 17:20). This one verse of Songs of Solomon 4:11 alone has many allegories of spiritual truth in it. The pine cone is another symbol used for the pineal gland. The sperm produced in the testicles is also produced by this spinal fluid. Before people started swearing with their hands over their hearts, they would place their hands on one's loins whom they were swearing to. It's where we get the words *testify* and *testimony* from. In Genesis 24:2–3, this custom was being portrayed by Abraham's servant.

All animal sacrifices are in line with this story as well. We are still talking about the Bible allegories of the zodiac, chakras, meditation, creation, plan of salvation, spirit, and our purpose. As I have said before, unless the sun enters or comes into Aries and burns up the sacrifice of the ram, spring cannot come. Unless you take no thought and watch or meditate and let your third eye or pineal gland be opened that the Spirit can purge the left side of the brain, that the virgin consciousness which allows God (Yahweh) to be born in you. The temple without hands, that the kingdom of God (Yahweh) can come. You can overcome through the spirit.

If this doesn't happen, you will never meet your purpose. You have no life in you.

Except ye eat the flesh of the Son of Man
and drink his blood, ye have not life in yourself.
(John 6:52)

In allegory, eating the flesh is killing the flesh. Blood represents life and spirit, which is real life being in you. Blood is red and represents emotions that I will talk about soon. Think about this: not meeting your purpose and not having life in you. You see, it doesn't matter how much you know about the Bible or how many churches you have under your belt.

Why call me Lord, Lord, and do not the
things that I say? (Luke 6:46)

In Matthew 6:33, "seek ye first the kingdom of God (Yahweh) and his righteousness"; that's what you do first. The kingdom is within you (Luke 17:20). That is what we're talking about. In Colossians 1:27, "Christ in you, the hope of glory." In 1 Corinthians 3:16–17, it tells you that you are the temple of God (Yahweh). So you can't defile the temple, you must hold it in high regard. Now keep this in mind: you are also the sacrifice. That is the all great amount of 10 percent of all that you are. And it is all that you are. Because it has been proven that we only use 10 percent of our minds.

Looking around, I think many use less. In Deuteronomy 6:5:

Thou shall love the Lord (Yahweh) thy God
(Elohim or mighty one) with all thine heart and
with all of thy soul and with all of thy might.

What else is there? That's everything! Yes, it is everything. In fact, it's all that we are. Yes, but it's still only 10 percent. It is 90 percent that we have no clue about.

Bring ye the whole tithes into the storehouse,
that there may be meat in my house and prove me
now herewith, said the LORD (Yahweh) of hosts,

> if I will not open you the window of heaven and
> pour you out a blessing, that there shall not be
> room enough to receive it. (Malachi 3:10)

Many think that this tithing is giving money to the church or 10 percent of your income. We have been brainwashed to believe that. No, the 10 percent is all that you are. Everything belongs to God (Yahweh) anyway. What is the allegory here? Well, where is the storehouse? In Matthew 6:19–20, treasures are in heaven. Meat in my house? Where is that? The kingdom of God (Yahweh) is in you. If I will not open you the window of heaven, in other words, you give all that you are, that little 10 percent, and Yahweh (God) will give you the 90 percent. Now how do you give this "that you are"? By not taking thought, by not being, by giving up your time, and by using his time. The Sabbath, the seventh—that's why it's holy. The seven chakras are meditation. That's what it pictures. That's why in John 21:6, he said, "Cast the net to the right side of the boat and ye shall find."

Find what? Fish. Picture God (Yahweh). That's why the big fish saves Jonah. After they listened to Yahshua (Jesus), how many fish did they find? They found 153 fish. That's one plus five plus three, which equals nine, the number of consciousness through the seven chakras of meditation. God (Yahweh) doesn't need your money (Haggai 2:8).

> The silver is mine, and the gold is mine,
> said the LORD (Yahweh) of hosts (1 Kings 20:3)

It all belongs to him anyway. With offerings, somewhere along the line, sacrifices were made. Human sacrifices of virgin women and small children. Then it was rams, goats, lambs, bullocks, and the list goes on. Why? What does the Bible say about this?

> To what purpose is the multitude of your
> sacrifices unto me? saith (Yahweh) the Lord, I am
> full of the burnt offerings of rams and the fat of
> fed beasts, and I delight not in the blood of bull-
> ocks or of lambs or of he-goats. (Isaiah 1:11)

Isaiah 1:13 tells how it's "an oblation and it is an abomination unto me." It's because it's religion. They took this stuff literally, and they missed the whole point. You see, blood is red, and it symbolizes emotion and most of the time the lower mind. That's why in allegory, they sprinkle blood here and there, and it was a Red Sea that the Israelites went through. It was also a red heifer that was used as a sacrifice. The devil is red, and Santa Claus is red. He also had a red suit on. Now I don't think anyone has really sat down and thought about this, but here it goes.

You have a Creator that has made everything that has ever been. He knows all the stars by name and he is full of love and is love. There is nothing hid in his eyes, and there is nothing that's too hard for him. He's all-powerful, all-merciful, all-wise, but the only trouble is the only thing in the universe He can come up with to forgive us is to kill innocent animals. Yet this wasn't good enough, so all the spilt blood for thousands of years was all for nothing, and He's all-knowing, so He already knew this. The scriptures said from the foundation of the world, Christ (Yahshua) would come and die for the sins of the world. So why kill innocent animals and command us to do it in the first place?

I don't mean any harm, but this sounds pretty stupid. Even believing this is an insult to your Creator. I don't believe it! It doesn't even make sense. I could see people doing this, but God (Yahweh) knows the end from the beginning. What was He trying to prove? This is the worst case of animal abuse you could possibly imagine.

So as I have said, Christ would die for the sins of the world. This I believe, but not in the way that most would think, basically because religious people don't. Christ (Yahshua) died at Calvary. Well, in Latin it's *calvaria*, in Greek, it's *kranion*, and in English, it's *cranium*, meaning skull. Even "Golgotha," the place of the skull. Christ (Yahshua) was the *testator*, which shows him dying for you, but even the word *testa* means skull. This is where the crucifixion takes place.

If Christ is in you, the body is dead because
of sin, but the spirit is life because of righteousness. (Romans 8:10)

> In that day ye shall know that I am in my
> father, and ye in me, and I in you. (John 14:20)

This is the reason for Christ's (Yahshua) life and is the reason for his death. This entails dying for the sins of the world. It's more symbolic than that. It's more spiritual than just that.

I'll start where I left off. It wasn't good enough killing all those innocent animals, so he (Yahweh, God) sends His Son down here and has us kill Him. Well, worse than just killing Him. I mean the worst killing you can ever imagine. He was beaten more than any man, mocked more than any man, humiliated more than any man, despised, rejected, hated, and the list goes on. His father could have stopped this at any time. Well, He (Jesus, Yahshua) could have stopped it. He could have just died and got the job done. He would have still died for our sins. No, it was a long ordeal, a whole lot longer than it had to have been. Why? Why the suffering on and on?

Now let's get this straight, this is God's will. His Son had to go through this long ordeal, which means something else that most people never think about. We know "Thou shall not kill" (In Ecclesiastes 3:3, "There's a time to kill, a time for every purpose under heaven"). I think it means "Thou shall not murder." That's killing for no reason, but that's what happened to Jesus (Yahshua). He was murdered and was done that way by a mob. Yet that was God's (Yahweh) will. Now that means if you were living there at that time and you tried to stop this in any way, shape, or form, you would have been going against God's (Yahweh) will.

Now, Judas and, don't forget, Pilate and the chief priests at the time and the Roman soldier that stuck that sword in his side, they get a bad rap. But if you think about it, they were actually doing God's (Yahweh) will. Do you see that this doesn't sound right? I'm not saying it didn't happen; at best, some things don't add up. What I am saying is that there's more to this story than meets the eye. It's symbolic. Yahshua (Jesus) never calls himself the Son of God; it's always the Son of Man. In allegory, He was showing that man, or us, just as Christ, or being Christ, had to die. We had to be the ram or the burnt offering ourselves.

Something else to note is killing the flesh spiritually is hard, and it is a long, drawn-out ordeal. Spiritually speaking, it's the same as what Christ (Yahshua) had to endure. It's the whipping down and the tearing of the flesh, not physically but mentally, emotionally, and spiritually. The mocking down of your perceptions, your vanity, and ego. Yet you can't do it; even thinking you can proves that you can't. You can't kill the physical (flesh), that's what you are. It's the fire (spirit) that burns up the physical. That's why it's a burnt offering; in allegory, that's what it pictures. You are to be the sacrifice. The whole creation tells us this.

The ancient Egyptians knew this. The Sphinx, being one of the seven wonders of the world, has a woman's head and a lion's body. The woman's head represents the constellation Virgo, and the lion's body represents the constellation Leo. Virgo the virgin, which you know by now by the many virgins of religions and the virgin births, is the pure consciousness that Christ can be born in us. The death of the sun (son) is Capricorn and its birth. Then by Aries, the sun (son) becomes the ram (lamb) or sacrifice, which we know is us, which is what's meant by the lion lying down with the lamb.

The sun or fire burns up the burnt offering by Leo, which is a fixed fire sign. The offering is burned up. Then it starts all over again in Virgo. This has been going on for eternity. The Bible was written in the sky long before it was ever written down on paper. The zodiac also shows the seven chakras and the overcoming of each. Then it shows the seventh chakra when you are the sacrifice.

The last four of the constellations show the four attributes of intellect. It starts with Virgo, the virgin, which is no thoughts, virgin consciousness. Through consciousness, you learn justice, which is the scales of justice; that is balance. This is Libra. Scorpio is the evils of yourself and the world, which you also learn. Sagittarius, the horse and man with an arrow, is direction, wisdom as you go up the chakras. Capricorn, the goat, the stubbornness needed and the will of climbing, which is what a goat does. Having one's heart into something—where does that saying come from? Goats are also used on the Day of Atonement as the sacrifice of us and Satan, or better yet, our emotional nature, which the heart always pictures—the feelings, love, and emotions, which is the heart chakra.

Then you have Aquarius, the man with the pitcher of water that pictures truth, water baptism, and the second stage of consciousness. It's also the new age, the throat chakra, the speaking of truth. Pisces shows the two fishes. Fish represents God (Yahweh), as Jonah was swallowed by the large fish. Jesus (Yahshua) was said to cast the nets to the right side to find fish. In Matthew 14:14–21, Christ (Yahshua) feeds five thousand people with five loaves and two fishes. In Matthew 15:32–38, four thousand are fed with seven loaves and a few little fishes. When you add the people together, it comes to nine thousand, and nine is the number of consciousness. The five loaves are the five stages of consciousness and also the five senses. The other seven loaves represent the seven chakras, which brings the intervention of the two fish as one can pull downward and the other upwards.

Our human spirit must be in line with also the pineal and pituitary glands, the two that bear witness in heaven and earth, candlesticks, lampstands, which I will talk about later. This is the sixth chakra or waterpot before the seventh, which in allegory must be filled before the seventh so that they all can be made wine (spirit). Then the last chakra, the crown, Aries, the ram, the complete sacrifice of you, which is the burnt offering. What is to be sacrificed is the four last constellations, which are the four attributes of man, that of physical (Taurus the bull). The power of the bull is what goes along with the plowing of the fields, even so far as representing us. Gemini, the twins, is our emotional nature, which is going back and forth, switching from one thing to another as the state of emotions does.

It's Cancer, the crab, which holds to things as our intellect does. That is our intellectual nature as the west pushes out the sun that rises in the east. Intellect pushes out spirit every time. Remember, spirit comes from the right side. Then there's Leo, the lion, the strongest of all beasts. The king of the jungle. It represents Christ (Yahweh), the Lion of the tribe of Judah. The King of kings. A king always has a crown, which is what the seventh chakra is called, the crown chakra; Judah was on the right side.

This is astronomy, which is all throughout the Bible. This is the Bible, written down before time. It's the whole plan of salvation. It's our whole purpose for being. It's the way, which zodiac means: "the way." It's the seven chakras. It's you. It's the way you work.

Astronomy is all throughout the Bible. Let's talk about a star called Venus. It's called the goddess of love. It's also called the morning star, but in ancient times, it was called something else. Venus was called Lucifer, the light-bearer. In the fall, the way the earth would tip would make the stars change position, and Venus became the evening star. It's like it crowds the sun back. This is Lucifer. In the fall, the star appears to fall. That may be how the fall got its name. In the spring and summer, this star is called Venus. Now Lucifer, by fundamentalists, is an angel that rebels and is cast to the earth. What is interesting about a star is the drawing of it. It has five points to it, which I will talk about soon.

In Isaiah 14:12:

> How art thou fallen from heaven, O Lucifer, son of the morning, how art thou cut down to the ground, which didst weaken the nations. For thou hast said in thine heart, I will ascend into heaven, I will exalt my throne above the stars of God, I will sit also upon the mount of the congregation, in the sides of the north. I will ascend above the heights of the clouds, I will be like the most high.

In mysticism, they would repeat a word or a theme over and over several times to emphasize a point. As I've said before, a star has five points. If you'll notice, *I* is written five times in these verses, showing the I as one's self, which has five senses. The lower mind or consciousness, the natural mind or carnal mind, which in Romans 8:7, can't be subject to the law of God (Yahweh). Now I'm not saying Lucifer is not just that because in Ezekiel 28:14, Lucifer is called a cherub that covereth. Now Satan is a play off the word Saturn. Saturn is also Cronus, which means time. "Father Time" is what he is referred to on first of the year, New Year's Day. "Old Man Time" is another term we use for him. He's an old gray-bearded man who has children around him and a sickle in his hands. We get the concept of Santa with the children sitting on his lap. We also get the concept of the "Grim Reaper."

Thousands of years ago, children were being sacrificed to this same god, which has several names: Molech, Moloch, Milcom, Malcham, even Chemosh for the Moabites. Baal was the name for Molech for Israel and where we get the name Lord from when we transliterate the word *Baal*. Also, Seth translates to Triton, to what we call a typhoon. All these names have formed the name Saturn and/or Satan. We said in Ezekiel 28:14 that Lucifer was a "cherub that covereth. He walks up and down the stones of fire, and he was in the Holy Mountain of God (Yahweh)." In allegory, it's both or one of the same thing, in the mind, where the kingdom of God is (Luke 17:20). The kingdom of heaven is above as within. As Venus is in the east or (right) in the spring and summer, where life is, it becomes Lucifer in the winter (left) where death is. The stones of fire are referring to the pineal and pituitary glands, where the fire or spirit of God resides.

In history, there are over twenty-one major saviors, but yet one is the right one? This is what Lyman Stone wrote in the late 1800s: "There are also many religions, but yet one is the right one? Or are they all just allegories of the same one true God?" Then he makes his last statement, which is that "astronomy is the basics of all religions."

The famous world-renowned father of medicine, Hippocrates, who was a Greek physician responsible for the "Hippocratic Oath," said a doctor that doesn't have a full understanding of astronomy has no right to call himself a doctor. That's because many people that are sick are sick because of nothing that is earthly. The stars affect us. It's a knowledge that is lost today.

Canst thou bind the cluster of Pleiades or
loose the bands of Orion? (Job 38:31)

The sun is born every year on December 25 in a stable. Why in a stable? Because it's between a horse and a goat or between Sagittarius and Capricorn. Astronomers use a day for a year, and so does the Bible. Now a point to look at is thirty years after Jesus (Yahshua) was born, He was baptized. Now thirty days after December 25 (when the sun was born), the sun enters into Aquarius (the water-bearer). That's not all. The next thing that happens is Jesus (Yahshua) picks out His disciples, who are fishermen. After Aquarius, the sun enters Pisces. Then Jesus (Yahshua) becomes the good shepherd, giving His life for the sheep. The sun enters into Aries (the ram) to be sacrificed, so that spring can come. The ram of God and the lamb of God give life to the world. That new life can be in you. The sun enters into Taurus (the bull), which represents agriculture. Now the fields are fit for plowing. The sun warms the earth for harvest. Inside you, the growth begins of the Spirit as well. The sun next enters into the constellation Gemini.

The Bible tells you that Paul was a Gemini. I will show you where astronomy is directly used in the Bible. Gemini has two stars in it called the two twins, Castor and Pollux. Now Paul, in Acts 28:1, said, "After three months we departed in a ship of Alexandria which had wintered in the isle, whose sign was Castor and Pollux."

By reason in mythology, a ship represents a person as being a vessel. If you remember, Jonah was in a ship and he had to be thrown off of in order for God (the big fish) to save him. Being a ship of Alexandria means he was from there, being in Rome. Paul was a Roman. He wintered there. By astronomy, winter's days are shorter, having less light. Paul, whose name was changed from Saul, had to be enlightened because he was in darkness. He had to be blinded so that he could truly see, whose sign was Castor and Pollux shows that he was a Gemini. Now leaving Gemini, the sun enters Cancer the crab. The vegetation starts to dry up and retreat outward. It's where the word *crabgrass* comes from.

Now it's Leo coming into August. Leo is a fire sign, and it's the hottest time of summer. The constellation of the lion has what is called the Dog Star in it, which explains where the dog days of summer come from in August. Then the sun starts over again in Virgo.

Now some of the constellations we haven't touched on yet are after Virgo. We know the virgin consciousness, then comes Libra. If you look at Isaiah 9:6–7, after the birth of Christ (Yahshua):

> Unto us a child is born, unto us a son is given. The government shall be upon his shoulder: and his name shall be called Wonderful, Counsellor, Mighty God, Everlasting Father, Prince of Peace. Of the increase of his government and of peace there shall be no end, upon the throne of David, and upon his kingdom, to establish it, and uphold it with judgment and with righteousness from henceforth even forever. The zeal of the LORD of hosts (Yahweh) shall perform this.

Libra has the scales of justice, the government being on his shoulders, and with judgment and righteousness forever. This is what Libra (the scales of justice) represents, Christ in you (Yahshua), which writes God's (Yahweh) laws on our hearts. Christ lived a perfect life, keeping God's (Yahweh) laws. Next, when the sun enters the constellation Scorpio, which is the betrayer (showing Judas), it sets the stage for the crucifixion. Sagittarius (the horseman with a bow) shows wisdom and the aiming and straightness of it. Capricorn is the goat (the goat is used to represent the devil in sacrifices). The stable used in the Bible for Christ's (Yahshua) birth shows the time of year he was born, between the horse and the goat. We have talked about Aquarius, which represents when the water was turned into wine at a wedding, and afterward, Christ (Yahshua) chooses his disciples (who were fishermen). Pisces, the two fish represent this.

The way (the zodiac) is but salvation in allegory, where Christ's (Yahweh) consciousness can be born in you, if you take no thought and enter into meditation or the single eye, and the energy up through the chakras touches the pineal gland and opens the right side of the brain that the spirit can purge or burn up the sacrifice. The 10 percent that you are. The life that truly is, is through the Christ

(Yahshua); He is your life. This is the allegory of what that means. The true you, the 90 percent, the prodigal son that, has come home. I will talk about this later.

The tree that we are eating from is a corrupt tree. We have been reaping from the outcome of it for thousands of years. The knowledge of the tree of good and evil must be destroyed. There's a story in allegory about this tree in the Bible that few see and understand. The story is in Matthew 21:18–19:

> Now in the morning, as he returned into the city, he hungered. And when he saw a fig tree in the way, he came to it and found nothing thereon but leaves only, and said unto it, "Let no fruit grow on thee henceforward forever." And presently the fig tree withered away.

Now if you would look at this at face value, it would appear that Christ (Yahshua) was walking somewhere, became hungry, saw a fig tree with only leaves and no figs, and he became angry and zaps the tree. The tree dies. Now take time to think about this for a moment. This is the Son of God (Yahweh) who is called the Prince of Peace, who is going to save the whole world. He walks on water. He gives sight to the blind. He heals the sick, and he even raises the dead. He commands demons, and all nature obeys him, and all power is given to him in heaven and earth. Yet he can't handle a fig tree not having figs. No, I'm not mocking the Bible nor am I saying that this didn't happen. What I am saying is, why is this written in the Bible? What is its spiritual significance? Not only that, it's like if I'm not going to have a fig, then no one is going to have a fig!

Now in the religious world, some believe that God is going to drop atomic bombs and bring world peace in that order, but does that even sound right. In Matthew 21:17–18, he was in Bethany. The city of Bethany means "city of" or "house of dates." Bethany was known for its date palm trees, which gave wonderful shade. All in the region knew this and would come for miles to escape the heat of the desert. Jesus (Yahshua) knew this as well. In allegory, this is saying the heat (or trials) of life needs to have shade, a refuge, a place to be restored, a safe haven to restore one's spirit to life again.

Many churches are named "Bethany" for the meaning of this word. Now, in the morning, the city has meanings after being in the shade and having one's spirit restored. He (Christ Yahshua) entered into the city (which in allegory is his consciousness), and the light is shining through meditation. He is hungry in his spirit to take in these truths and start anew. He is active in the spirit, the light, the bright and morning star. The great city is consciousness.

In Hebrews 12:22, "But ye have come unto Zion, and unto the city of the living God, the heavenly Jerusalem." This hunger is not of food.

In Matthew 15:11, "It's not what goes into a man that defiles him, but what comes out of him."

In Matthew 5:6, "Blessed are those who hunger and thirst after righteousness, for they shall be filled."

In Psalm 107:9, "For he satisfieth the longing soul, and filleth the hungry soul with goodness." This is what the spirit does.

One thing, first of all, Yahshua (Jesus) would not harm any living creature. Now what is this all about? What is the teaching here? In Matthew 21:19, he saw the fig tree in the way. This is throughout the New Testament. In Matthew 21:8, multitudes spread their garments in the way. In Acts 9:17, Ananias went his way and entered into the house and, putting his hands on him, said, "Brother Saul, the Lord, even Jesus (Yahshua) that appeared unto thee in the way."

In Isaiah 35:8, "A highway shall be there, and a way, and it shall be called the way of holiness; the unclean shall not pass over it."

In Matthew 7:14, "Enter the straight gate, for straight is the gate and narrow is the way that leads unto eternal life." The way is internal. Paul was knocked off his horse. Remember that a horse is wisdom in mythology and allegory. Paul had to be knocked off his horse, his wisdom, his knowledge, and understanding in order to follow the way. In 1 Corinthians 1:11, "Be ye followers of me, even as I also am of Christ (Yahshua)."

"Me" is "I am," and "I am" is the way. The way is inside you through meditation.

> I am the way, the truth, and the life. John 14:6)

Paul was blinded for three days and nights, showing the death of his way or old life. The zodiac does not come from the word *zoo*, as many believe, but from the word *the-o or zz-o*, which means "the way." The way is meditation. In Hebrews 10:19:

> Having therefore, brethren, boldness to enter into the holiest by the blood of Jesus (Yahshua), by a new and living way, which he had consecrated for us, through the veil, that is to say, his flesh.

They're still looking for the holiest of holies over in the Holy Land, Jerusalem, or somewhere. Yet it's inside you. Now back to the fig tree. When you are in the way and the door is opened to the right side, the first thing, symbolically Christ (Yahshua), looks for is fruit. In Matthew 7:16 and 20, "Ye shall know them by their fruit."

Galatians 5:22 talks about the fruit of the spirit. Now the reason it's a fig tree is because a fig blooms from the inside, not the outside. That's your treasure in heaven. That's your pearl of great price. In Revelation 2:7, "To him who overcomes will I give to eat of the tree of life." Now we have been eating of the tree of the knowledge of good and evil.

In Genesis 2:17, "But of the tree of the knowledge of good and evil, thou shalt not eat of it; for in the day that thou eatest thereof thou shalt surely die."

In Psalm 1:3, "He shall be like a tree planted by the rivers of water, that brings forth fruit in his season; his leaf also shall not wither, and whatsoever he doeth shall prosper."

Christ (Yahshua) is coming for your fig tree. This is the tree of life, your higher mind. The tree of the knowledge of good and evil is the lower mind. It only, in most cases, has leaves that block out the light of God (Yahweh). If it has any fruits, they are bad fruits. In Matthew 7:18, "A good tree cannot bring forth evil fruit, neither can a corrupt tree bring forth good fruit."

So, in Matthew 21:19, when Christ (Yahshua) says, "Let no fruit grow on thee henceforward forever," He is talking about the corrupt tree, the tree of the knowledge of good and evil. The fruit of that tree will never hurt you again but will die.

In the concept of one, there are many because we are all individuals, with our own backgrounds and understandings. Yet we are all that one being because of our being. We have a shared space, and we share our being in that space. We have the same means of consciousness in that space. Our hurt is the same hurt of others, and our joy is the same as others. Yet we seek our differences and compare our joys and failures and see to our own as if we truly had our own. We find that the only care that we can possibly have is that of others. We see as if we can and can only find our blindness.

Have you ever noticed that the word *eye* and the letter *I* sound the same but don't look the same? And the letter *I* and the number *1* (one) look the same but don't sound the same? Yet all three are the same identical thing. *There's a reason.* In the deep stages of consciousness, when the light of the divine is within, there's a peace and a unity beyond anything known. There is a connection with all things that you are and that you are well aware of being a part of. *At that point*, all the different *I*s or eyes are actually 1 (one), and you are the same. There is no division between anything. What love is, you are, and what God is, you are. What your fellow man is, you are as well.

It's hard to explain the warmth and the care, nor the power and wisdom that is going through you. You are a conduit of the Master as well as His very voice and being. Yet we are as sheep that have gone astray. We sit in darkness and see not the light that is in us.

Jesus (Yahshua) walks on the water. Why is that in the Bible? Is it just a story to tell? What is its spiritual significance? What does it teach? In Matthew 14:22, after five thousand men, besides women, and children were fed, Jesus (Yahshua) straightway constrained His disciples to get in a ship and to go before Him unto the other side while He sent the multitudes away. In verse 23, He went up into a mountain apart to pray. When the evening was come, He was there alone.

In verse 24, the ship was now in the midst of the sea, tossed with waves, for the wind was contrary. Verse 25 says, "And in the fourth watch of the night, Jesus went unto them walking on the sea. When his disciples saw him walking on the sea, they were troubled, saying, 'It is a spirit,' and they cried out for fear."

In verse 27, Jesus (Yahshua) straightway spoke unto them, saying, "Be of good cheer; it is I; be not afraid."

Peter, in verse 28, answered him and said, "Lord, if it be thou, bid me come unto thee on the water." Then Peter walked on the water.

When he saw the wind boisterous (blowing) and the waves, he took his eyes off Jesus (Yahshua) and began to sink. He cried out to Yahshua, and He saved him.

Now, in allegory, the ship is you. The five thousand show the five stages of consciousness. The disciples were told to go to the other side of the sea while the multitude was sent away. The other side is the higher stage of consciousness, which is the single eye or meditation. The multitude are the ones that are without, where things are done in parables (Matthew 4:11). Even his mother and brethren are standing without, where Jesus (Yahshua) asked, "Who is my mother?" etc. (Mark 3:31–33).

You can be stuck on religion or anything and not meditate and be without. Meditation is going within. While the multitude went away, Yahshua or Jesus goes up to a mountain to pray. This is referring to going into oneself or meditation. A mountain refers to the kingdom, and the kingdom is within you (Luke 17:20). This happens in the evening, the best time to meditate. Now the ship was tossed with waves and wind where the disciples were. Remember the ship is us. The wind and the waves are the trials, problems, and thoughts of this world.

The fourth watch is the fourfold nature or attributes of man: intellectual, emotional, spiritual, and physical. *Watch* refers to meditation. Jesus (Yahshua) comes walking on the water. Water always refers to truth. The disciples were troubled with fear, which had been planted in them by the world and its beliefs, superstitions, and teachings. When Jesus (Yahshua) said, "Fear not, for it is I," He was talking about the "I am." "I" is the "am" singular, and it refers to the "I am" that is in each of us. It makes you wonder where the "I" for us comes from.

Peter, who also walked on water, was named by Yahshua (Jesus). Peter means "little stone." The pineal gland is also called a little stone. Peter, who walked on water, is an allegory of the pineal gland being activated by spirit and truth (water). The distractions of waves and wind, which caused Peter to start to sink, are also the thoughts and distractions that stop the pineal gland from being activated to open up the right side of the brain. Jesus (Yahshua) saves Peter, even with his lack of faith.

Now, looking at this another way, which has been proven by quantum theory in physics, light as photons on the molecular level, even being called molecular particles or messenger particles, are the things that atoms are made of. They cannot be understood by any conventional means known to science. They are, by their own response, shown to have their own intelligence or consciousness. These photons have been split, blown up, radiated, and used in every test known to man, yet they can't be destroyed. When they are blown up, they only reappear close by. When they are split, they become two. What we have learned about them is safely guarded and kept from the general public, but you didn't hear that from me.

What we know about in Einstein's theory of relativity, along with the atomic bomb, $E=MC^2$, and the study of the universe and dark matter are as child's play or as learning your ABCs compared to what is on the quantum level, which is in each atom of each cell throughout the known universe. In theory, what was packed closely in one solid mass, trillions of times more than any known thing in the universe was through what is known as the Big Bang theory. What has been considered as a giant explosion, to say the least (which must have been controlled more than any explosion known), is still moving several times the speed of light in all directions. As recent as the last twenty years, it has been proven that all matter contained within its genetic codes consists of the same patterns of molecular development in all living things, that the same photons are seen in both plants and animals in that they coexist and communicate with one another and that there are no spaces in between. We were talking about how photons could not be destroyed.

In the splitting of the photons, what was found by separating them thousands of miles is that the reactions of one, due to an experiment done to another, are the same for both, even though they were separated by thousands of miles. Their reactions were synchronized in that they occurred at the same time. In other words, time and space do not exist in the molecular world. They seem to appear and go at random and from nowhere.

This information shows that we are not what we thought we were. Matter itself is not what we thought it was. We are linked together as in a grid or a force that connects all things as one. It's a collective consciousness or frequency in which all things vibrate. It goes along with John 1:1 that says, "In the beginning was the word, and the word was with God, and the word was God." (Word as a sound.)

The same was in the beginning with God. This shows this was from the beginning. In verses 4 and 5, "In him was life, and the life was the light of men. And the light shineth in darkness, and the darkness comprehended it not." In him was life (this is true life), and this true life was the light of men (sounds like it's photons), and remember, they can't be destroyed. It shines in darkness, and the darkness comprehends it not. The pineal gland works better in darkness; it's sensitive to light. There's a reason these photons (or light) exist in darkness and are the light of men.

The Word (sound or frequency) vibrates and was set out at the beginning of time in which all things consist, even life itself. All matter is atoms with electrons that flow around their nucleus, positive and negative charges which produce heat as with the laws of thermodynamics, and energy is created. From the photons or messenger particles (spirit) vibrations, matter is produced; well, what we know as matter for what we can or might perceive. Lightning falls from the sky, where it actually comes from the ground up. White as a color is really no color, and cold doesn't exist; it's only the absence of heat, and the list goes on. As we say "as blind as a bat," its perception is hundreds of times more than ours. From a particle of dust to a gnat, fifty yards in all directions, we are designed to see as we see and to hear as we hear. There are frequencies we don't know of as there are some we do, like microwaves and radio waves for TV and remote controls, etc. Dogs and other animals can hear frequencies we can't. It has been proven that even water exposed to different frequencies changes its molecular state. When more than one frequency is used, it becomes a pulse. The heartbeat is as a pulse and is used as the seat of feelings and emotions and is really how prayer works.

When many pray in a heartfelt way, something is going to happen. It's a fact that the heart has a magnetic field three times more than the brain. You have EKGs and EEGs to prove it. We know not the power that is within us. For we are energy and have orbs and power and forces unseen nor heard of but on the quantum level have been proven to exist. Through our conscious level, we produce energy as well, either positive or negative. That's the reason the same terms for energy in electrical terms are the same for conduct, behaviors, and attitudes, being positive or negative. Your emotions and feelings control such fields, which brings into existence your reality. That is what has been called the Law of Attraction.

The Bible calls it "What you sow, you shall reap" (Galatians 6:7).

As a man thinks, so is he (Proverbs 23:7).

The kingdom of God (Yahweh) is in you (Luke 17:20)

I am is in you. God (Yahweh), I am, is love. The love chapter in the Bible is 1 Corinthians 13. Now we see through a glass darkly; the word for glass in the *Strong's Concordance* is 2072, Greek *esoptron*, which means mirror. The way the law of attraction works is that it reflects back to you what you reflect to it. If you are always asking for something, "I need this. Please give me this or that," then the universe does the same thing back to you. The world and all the things around you become "I need this, I want that," and it will be taken from you. Mostly because it is what you reflected in the first place. Whereas if your heart is right, that's where those types of sayings come from,. "If it is in your heart" and so forth, then it will be. "How may I serve you? How may I help you?" If it's heartfelt, that's the energy, that's the feeling, that's the God (Yahweh) in you. Then the universe and all the things in it, because it's all from God (Yahweh), will reflect back to you. "How may I serve you? How may I help you?"

That's why it's more blessed to give than to receive (Acts 20:35). Without knowing it, whatsoever you ask in God's (mine) name (Yahweh), He (I) will do (John 14:13). Mine, me, I—all refer to "I am," which is what Yahweh means, "I am that I am." So when you say, "I am tired, I am sick, I am unhappy," you are not only taking God's or Yahweh's name in vain, you are also telling the universe what you want. You are also feeling sad and sick and depressed, and this makes an impact on your subconscious mind that this becomes your automatic way to react. You can reprogram your subconscious mind, the way you think, and the way you feel. With God (Yahweh), all things are possible (Matthew 19:26).

When you look at Romans 4:17, it reads, "Before him whom he believed God, who quickened the dead and calleth those things which be not as though they were," a knowing, which is spiritual and is not known intellectually, and is not even known through your own senses. So seeing the end result before it happens, or seeing the end from the beginning, is based on belief or faith. It's like it's backward from what is taught. The saying "I'll believe it when I see it" is really "I'll see it when I believe it."

Faith is the substance of things hoped for and
the evidence of things not seen. (Hebrews 11:1)

This is also not something you work up but is a gift of God (Yahweh) (Ephesians 2:8). It's a life force.

There's something you can do. Try this: each and every day, say this to yourself: (1) I accept my life now no matter how bad it is. (2) Yes, it may be hard now, but I'm gonna be okay; in fact, everything is going to be okay. (3) The "I am" that's in me is God (Yahweh), and nothing is too hard or impossible for Him, and I am and I know I am that I am, because He is, and I feel and see myself that I cannot fail but can only be victorious. When you say it, you begin to believe it, and if you believe it, then "it is." That's the truth. It's a universal law. You can and will control your reality; that is, if you don't let your reality control you.

Think about this: everything is consciousness used as frequencies which make up all things. As I have said before, on the molecular level of all things, they communicate with one another, and any changes to one is a change to them all. There is no space nor time. You are everything, and everything is you. You are gods, as John 10:34 reads. Science has even proven it. That's why any judgment on your part brings also conclusions on other parts, even without knowing it. Karma works and is the very way nature and all the universe balance itself out. A false balance is an abomination to the Lord (Yahweh) (Proverbs 11:1). A false balance could be doing something good for the wrong reason. A good balance might be something that doesn't seem that good or nice but is done for the right reason or is done for the greater good, which would result in good karma.

Now what regulates your karma is your chakras which connect you with the universe, Yahweh, God, the universal spirit, and this force and frequency. Now karma is the balancing out of positive and negative forces. How this force is used determines whether it's good or evil. The old saying "What goes around comes around" is as well "cause and effect." That is because you can't have your cake and eat it too. All these sayings or allegories explain how the life force works. All of our realities are in place because of our universal consciousness or mind, as it were. There is only one mind, and we are as many workers building his or her home.

We have built our world by our thoughts and emotions, which all stem from only two emotions: fear and love. From fear, we have greed, lust, jealousy, envy, hate, selfishness, pride, and doubt. This you can see if you look in Galatians 5:19. Now from love, you have joy, peace, kindness, gentleness, forgiveness, courage, faith, hope, and compassion as seen in verse 22. So, Yahweh God, or even your true self, you must know and control your thoughts and emotions. To know how your mind will be is to know what you are going to feed your mind, to know how you think.

There are a lot of people who believe a lot of crazy and different things. With this world standard, I'm one of them. I'm saying that you know can't be right. I mean, what they are believing and doing is so wrong and off base that it looks like the walls would come crashing down all around them. Yet they seem to be blessed. That is because we see their lack of understanding, and we see their understandings even as lies, and we know they're not true. What we don't see is their heart, and we don't see their love nor how much they serve others.

We think the truth makes us right with God (Yahweh), and it doesn't. Not in knowing it. Remember Romans 8:7, "the mind of man can't be right with God." Knowledge is puffed up, 1 Corinthians 8:1. Their kindness, faith, and compassion are spiritual, not intellectual. How much more are they in tune with this frequency of the universe? This God (Yahweh) called love? Karma—we have made it some other religion, but it's more than that. When Jesus (Yahshua) talked about "judge not, that ye be not judged" (Matthew 7:1), what was he talking about? Better yet, "if you judge yourself, you shall not be judged."

You really don't have any control of anything in this world. It's only your mind that you can have control of, and that's your emotions, passions, and impulses. Most don't have control of them and have never been taught to. Yet, in controlling them, you would have control over all things. Now not as the world would see. Let me explain. We have been taught guilt and fear, sin, good and evil, by everything we do. It's either good or evil. We have been taught fear by religion and also superstitions, all to control us by. You see, none of this is true. It's the way you think. You create your reality. If you believe something is wrong, it doesn't matter how right it is, it's still gonna be wrong, mostly due to the way that you think.

If you are thinking good things, you're not going to be doing bad things. Does that mean you're gonna do everything right? That you're not going to make some mistakes? No, it doesn't. You still may do some bad things. What I am saying is you can't do anything bad if you're in your right mind (I could go back to meditation, but if you have been reading so far, you'll know what I mean). A tree is known by its fruit, the vine; you're the branches (Matthew 7:16). The vine is eternal universal consciousness. Everything is connected to it. However, most don't know they are, so they are not by thinking they're not. "My people are destroyed for lack of knowledge" (Hosea 4:6).

We talked earlier about the flat earth and some things in the Bible that supported it. However, we haven't talked about practical information that supports it, that anyone can see if they would take an honest look at the facts. Let's look at the facts. An apple hits on Newton's so-called head, and gravity was discovered. You then had planets spinning around the earth and so-called formulas to support the theory, which would make sense on a spinning globe, but on a flat earth, why would you need gravity?

You have the earth spinning a thousand miles an hour, but we don't fly off because of this force. If this was true, how are we able to walk? Now on a spinning earth, you are moving with the earth, so I can see travel being possible. I can't see that in the air. You are not on the earth. You're flying seven hundred miles an hour on a plane, trying to land on a moving earth. You have a moon that you can see in the daytime, which seems to blend in with the sky, which doesn't cast any shadow of any kind on the ground, even though it's between the earth and the sun. Not only that, Mercury and Venus are planets between the earth and the sun, and they should never be seen at night, but they are. Even alongside Jupiter, which is on the other side of the earth.

Now another fact that has been overlooked is the sunrise. By the globe model, the earth is on a twenty-two-degree angle, and in the summertime, the northern hemisphere is closer to the sun. With the earth spinning clockwise, you, being on the earth, coming out of the darkness (night), the back of the earth to the front, the angle is downward, and by you going downward, looking at the sun, it appears to rise; thereby, we have sunrise. That makes sense.

What happens on the other side of the sun, when the northern hemisphere is furthest from the sun, and the sun is hitting on the southern hemisphere? You, being on the earth, would be on the other side of the planet, and coming out of the darkness into the light (morning), by the globe model, the rotation of the earth has not changed. You would be going up by the twenty-two-degree angle tilt of the earth, and the sun would appear to be going down until noon, when the sun would then appear to be going up. There's no debunking this. So by what we've been taught, it is impossible to have a sunrise in the Northern Hemisphere in the wintertime and also in the summer for the Southern Hemisphere.

Another fact is that with the circumference of the earth, there should be an eight-inch square drop per every mile to account for the globe. There isn't. You can see cities hundreds of miles away in the distance. A jet flying would have to continue going downward in flight not to fly off the planet. Ask any pilot, and they will tell you that you only level off and go straight. Any building of long bridges uses lasers and transits that are in a straight line, and no account for this eight-inch drop is considered. These are some things to consider. I'm not saying the earth is flat, but I can't see how it can be round. The fact that if we have been lied to, and if the truth is hidden from us that the earth and the universe are not what we think it is, what else have we been lied to about?

It said in 1 Thessalonians 5:21, "Prove all things, hold fast that which is good." I started with history and then the different religions. Then I went through the Bible with allegories, truth, and some facts. Now I have shown that even in science, the same truth and facts say the same things. That God (Yahweh) is one, that He's before all things, and He's in all things, and by Him, all things consist. The great "I Am," hallelujah! Let Him be praised forever and ever.

As I said before, the Bible is written in allegory. Religion has taken things literally. "As in the days of Noah, so shall the coming of the Son of Man be" (Matthew 24:37). The end-time refers to the end of the age. The end of Pisces the fish to the beginning of the Aquarius age, the man with the pitcher of water. In Luke 22:10, "Behold, when ye are entered into the city, a man there shall meet you bearing a pitcher of water, follow him into the house where he entereth in"; verse 11, "And ye shall say unto the goodman of the house, the master saith unto thee, where is the guest chamber where I shall eat the Passover with my disciples?" In verse 12, "And he shall show you a large upper room furnished, there make ready."

In Matthew 24:42, "Watch ye therefore, for ye know not what hour your Lord comes"; verse 44, "But know this, that if the goodman of the house had known in what watch the thief would come, he would have watched, and would not have suffered his house to be broken up." Keep this in mind as in the days of Noah.

For I will be getting back to that. The end of the world is really the end of an age, being Pisces. We are now in the age of Aquarius, which is shown to be, by astronomy, "the man with the pitcher of water." Water in allegory means truth and is also used to refer to spirit as being poured. In 1 John 5:6, "The spirit is truth." In Acts 2:17, "In the last days, I will pour my spirit upon all flesh."

Back to Luke 22:10, "When ye are entered into the city"; city in allegory means meditation (I will explain).

> Ye come unto Sion unto the city of the living God (Yahweh) the heavenly Jerusalem and to an innumerable company of angels. (Hebrews 12:22)

This is not something on this earth).

> The Kingdom of God (Yahweh) is in you. (Luke 17:20)

What else can this be but going inside yourself (Luke 11:52)?

Then it said, "A man shall meet you bearing a picture of water." At that time, you wouldn't find a man toting a pitcher of water; that was a woman's job. This is showing the Aquarius age.

Now putting this all together, it refers to the age we are now in. When you go into meditation (into the city) in the Aquarius age (man with the pitcher of water) or end-time, go into the house (yourself), go to the large upper room (which refers to your mind), the part you don't use, the 90 percent or right side we've talked about. This is the kingdom of God (Yahweh) that's in you (Luke 17:20). I will meet you there ("I" refers to I am.)

At this time, the Aquarius age, referred to as the end-times by most religions, is true if you know the symbols. Now in Matthew 24:42, when it refers to watch, it means meditate. Hour refers to Yahshua's (Christ) return at the age of Aquarius. In Revelation 3:10, the last part, "I will keep thee from the hour of temptation which shall come upon all the world to try them that dwell upon the earth." That is what is going on now with the water that is being poured by the man with the pitcher of water, being Aquarius.

The good man of the house is the God-man of the house or body or even his life. If he had known at what watch (time of meditation) the thief would come, this is the evil time, with the lower mind, and this strong energy that is being poured out (that if we are not prepared for it) would wipe us away. This is the temptation coming upon the whole world to try them. He would have watched or (meditated) that his house (life or being) would not be broken up or (destroyed).

> Remember therefore how thou hast received and heard, and hold fast and repent. If therefore thou shalt not watch, I will come on thee as a thief, and thou shalt not know what hour I will come upon thee. (Revelation 3:3)

So this thief is not Satan as the world believes, and you need to watch at this time for the Aquarius age, which is meditation. By meditation is how you receive and hear, not with your ears, physical, but with your spirit. This energy, which is from God, is not processed through the spirit with meditation; the result will be evil. Let me explain.

> There's no power but God (Yahweh) (Romans 13:1).

> I create evil and good. (Isaiah 45:7)

There is a duality in everything in the universe: left, right, hot, cold, life, death, peace and war, good and evil. The thing to note is left and right are two extremes of the same thing, and that is direction. Hot and cold are the extremes of temperature. Life and death are the extremes of existence that we've been taught. War and peace and good and evil are both based on the same source, and that is spirit. Energy, for example, for electricity in the right hands can light your homes; and in the wrong hands, it can burn your home down. Knowing about something and knowing how to use something are two different things. So this Aquarius age brings forth this pouring of the spirit resulting in the changes in this world.

Now I said to keep this in mind. As in the days of Noah, they were eating and drinking, marrying, and giving in marriage until the day that Noah entered the Ark (Matthew 24:38). Not that this is bad by itself, but it is still all physical. In Matthew 4:4, "Man doesn't live by bread alone but by every word that proceeded out of the mouth of God."

In John 6:35, "I am the bread of life." It's spiritual food and even drink.

> If any man thirst let him come unto me.
> (John 7:37)

> Be glad and rejoice and give honor to him
> for the marriage of the Lamb is come and his wife
> hath made herself ready. (Revelation 19:7)

We are to be ready for marriage to the Lamb or spiritual Christ (Yahshua). In Noah's time, it was the end of the world (age) also. The world then was to be ended by water—Aquarius is the water-bearer. Remember that water is truth and spirit. Spirit is also referred to as fire.

> When Pentecost was fully come, there
> appeared unto them cloven tongues like as of
> fire. All were filled with the Holy Ghost (spirit).
> (Acts 2:3)

When the waters (rains) came down in Noah's days, the only way he was saved was to go into an ark. In our day, as the water comes from Aquarius, the water-bearer as truth and spirit, which represents fire, the only way we can be saved is by going into our ark, which is inside of ourselves in our minds in meditation. Now on the ark were two of every animal, male and female, and seven of the clean animals. Now we already know by allegory that male represents the physical, ego, and intellect. The female represents the emotional and spiritual. The seventh of the animals that can be by the intervention of God (Yahweh) through meditation changed. Seven always shows the intervention of God (Yahweh); in this case all of the intervention would be done through the seven chakras.

The animals are in the ark with Noah as our thoughts and animal nature in us. We survive the flood by having our ark (minds and being) rest upon the waters (truth and spirit).

> He is like a man that built a house (his life),
> and dug deep and laid the foundation on a rock
> (meditation and the pineal gland): and when the
> flood arose, the stream beat vehemently upon that
> house and could not shake it: for it was founded
> upon a rock. (Luke 6:48 and also Matthew 7:24)

Religions show the rock being Christ (Yahshua), which is true except more can be said about this, the "I am" that Yahshua said, "I am the way the truth and the life" (John 14:6). The "I am" which is in you, through meditation, the pineal gland, becomes hard (like a stone or rock) when used by "the way," which has been said before is meditation. The ark resting on the seventh month on a mountain also shows the seven chakras and the mountain, being the kingdom that's in you or the higher mind or Christ's (Yahshua) consciousness.

Now meditation, where energy comes up the spine and touches the pineal gland and opens the right hemisphere of the brain and spirit can purge your whole being. This is a strange teaching for any Christian in our way of religion. Yet this is taught and practiced in every other religion on the face of the earth except ours. Why is that? There are stages of consciousness taught in this, which are the same in most all cultures. It is, from the first or bottom up to the top: earth, water, air, fire, and divine mind.

In 1 Thessalonians 4:17, "Then we which are alive and remain shall be caught up together with them in the clouds to meet the Lord in the air, and so shall we ever be with the Lord." This by most religions is the rapture, but the Word is not even in the Bible. The air is the third stage of consciousness (1 Thessalonians 4:16). "And the trump of God (Yahweh) referring to the last trump or trumpet" (Revelation 8:2). There are seven angels with seven trumpets.

> I saw heaven opened and behold a white
> horse. (Revelation 19:11)

What is interesting about this horse is that it is in your mind. You have what is called the hippocampus, which is known as the white horse. The sixth chakra, the pineal gland or the Ajna chakra, which is called Ammon's ram in which the children of Israel used the ram's horn as a trumpet in battles and warnings, also in starting holy days and feasts. Now this is referring to your mind or what's inside you. Look back at your house being built upon a rock; remember, this is the condition of your pineal gland when used. Now more is told in this allegory or parable in Matthew 7:24: "Not everyone has ears to hear, so keeping these sayings of mine or (me, I, I am, the God (Yahweh) within) is like a wise man building his house on a rock. The foolish man built his house (life or being) upon the sand."

When the pineal gland is not used or activated, it stays in a sandy state or condition. In the Aquarius age, as I have been saying, consciousness shall be affected more and more. You can either adapt to it (which can only be done through meditation) or you can resist it. However, this force or energy can only come one of two ways, either as a negative or a positive energy. Very few know this, and that's why it is said it is as a thief in the night, and most won't even know that it came.

Matthew 24:40 and Luke 17:34 talk about two being in a field, and one shall be taken and the other left. Then it said two women shall be grinding at the mill, and one shall be taken and the other left. Now in Luke 17:34, it said that in that night, there shall be two men in one bed, and one shall be taken and one left. Now what is the likelihood of that? This is allegory. Remember the two animals, either male or female, that were put into the ark? Do you notice that in all these examples, you have two being either in a field or in a mill or even a bed?

Now, in this case, it's either two males together or it's two women together. Women are the emotions or spirit. You have a lower mind or higher mind, a lower consciousness, worldly, lustful, selfish, and evil. Or you can, through the spirit, have a high Christ (Yahshua) consciousness, which has killed the lower mind through the spirit. Now male is the intellect and the ego, the knowledge of the tree of good and evil, but not the spiritual wisdom to know the difference. Now one of these is going to be taken and the other left. Now this is gonna happen in the Aquarius age.

In the last days perilous times shall come.
(2 Timothy 3:1)

And it gives a long list of what is going on now because of the Aquarius age. Evil men and seducers shall wax worse and worse, deceiving and being deceived. War and rumors of war, Matthew 24:6

says. Nature itself is affected with this Aquarius age. The hurricanes, earthquakes, and natural disasters increase more and more. It is the violence, killings, hate, greed, and emotional turmoil along with immorality and corruption that increase each passing day.

The seventh month, in which I started this book, picture this time with the prophecy of the first day of the seventh month being trumpets, when the ram's horn was blown. The Aquarius age comes in as war. The holy days are rehearsals for that coming event. To not know the hour is to explain this holy day. For you have to wait or watch for the new moon, which begins the seventh month. In meditation, you have no thoughts, so you wait and watch. Then comes the oneness, the atonement, when you become at one with God (Yahweh).

Atonement has the two goats, which by religious means pictures Jesus (Yahshua) and Satan, the devil. The only thing about this is everywhere else in the Bible where Christ (Yahshua) is pictured, it is as a lion of the tribe of Judah or as the lamb of God (Yahweh), the Alpha and Omega, the Son of the Highest, King of kings, Prince of *Peace*, and so on, but never as a goat, an unruly animal, hardheaded and stubborn. In Leviticus 16:7, one of the goats, after casting lots, was killed and its blood sprinkled on the altar seven times. Now atonement was made for it, and all the sins are placed on the live goat. The live goat is sent into the wilderness by the hand of a strong man.

Now the allegory is that the two goats are one and the same. It pictures our lower nature or mind. There's a fire by the altar, and there's blood, and blood is red, showing spirit and emotion. The blood sprinkled seven times is the seven chakras, which is placed on the live goat, which is now controlled by a strong man. The goat is led into the wilderness; that is, meditation. One goat had to die, which is us, the part that needed to die, but the live goat is us as well. It is saved by the spirit (blood) and is now controlled by the strong man (God or Yahweh) through meditation.

Or else you believe, at face value, the live goat which has all the sins of the whole world placed back on it from the dead goat is allowed to live, while the other goat which had atoned for sin was killed for no reason. How can the live goat be Satan and the dead goat be Jesus (Yahshua)? Nothing is said about the dead goat coming back alive again through a resurrection.

The wages of sin is death. (Romans 6:23)

Now all the sins of the dead goat were placed on the live one. Yet no more is said about the live goat. This is an allegory. Both goats are you. The question is, which one are you going to kill or sacrifice through the seven chakras to kill the carnal mind or the other to be controlled by a strong man (Yahshua), Jesus or God, led into the wilderness of meditation?

The Feast of Tabernacles for seven days is that wilderness of meditation or the seven chakras. We are temporary dwellings, that's all we are; well, that's all our bodies are. Year after year, you would make these temporary dwellings. Why? Because it takes many lifetimes, who knows how many? You had the choice each time of what your temporary dwelling would be. Yet you don't know this because each time was new. Yet there's no new thing under the sun (Ecclesiastes 1:9).

The seven chakras called "*Shasara*" is represented as having one thousand petals as Christ (Yahshua) sets up his kingdom for a thousand years. Revelation 20:11 shows a Great White Throne. In Revelation 20:4, the last part: "and they lived and reigned with Christ (Yahshua) a thousand years."

The Feast of Tabernacles, also called the Feast of Booths, or as has been said, "temporary dwellings," shows the biggest secret in life, and that is this isn't life. It's a temporary dwelling. The real-life part of us is what we don't see. A prophecy in Isaiah 11:9 I thought was an outside event, which I later learned is an inside (spirit) event to be transformed to the outside. The earth shall be full of the knowledge of the Lord (Yahweh) as the waters cover the sea.

I'm not saying the kingdom is not coming. I'm saying it is coming in this "Aquarius age." It is already here. Consciousness has to be changed. It's through the pouring of the spirit by this water-bearer that this is being done.

> Flesh and blood cannot inherit the kingdom
> of God nor does corruption inherit incorruption.
> (1 Corinthians 15:50)

This way or "the way" we have said about the way is through the gospel of the kingdom of Yahweh God which is in you (Luke 17:20). It's the seven chakras and meditation and prayer (which is part of meditation), the upper room with the man with the pitcher of water (which is "the way").

> And this gospel of the kingdom shall be
> preached to the whole world for a witness unto all
> nations and then shall the end come. (Matthew
> 24:14)

Do you think this is a story about Christ (Yahshua)? This is a story about "the way."

> And Jesus (Yahshua) went into the temple
> of God (Yahweh) and cast out all them that sold
> and bought in the temple, and overthrew the
> tables of the money changers and the seats of
> them that sold doves. (Matthew 21:12)

> Know ye not that ye are the temple of God
> (Yahweh) and that the spirit of God (Yahweh)
> dwelleth in you?, If any man defile the temple of
> God (Yahweh), him shall God (Yahweh) destroy;
> for the temple of God (Yahweh) is holy, which
> temple ye are. (1 Corinthians 3:16–17)

When Jesus (Yahshua) went into the temple in Matthew 21:12, he wasn't talking about going into a church. In Matthew 24:2, he said there shall not be left one stone upon another that would not be cast down. This is an allegory. This is not a physical temple. This is the temple made without hands. Jesus (Yahshua) enters your temple (your mind). He casts out all them that sold and bought in the temple, which would be your thoughts, desires of the flesh, and lower mind, which is obsessed with gain and will always want more and more material things. The real hell, the bottomless pit, this desire that never has enough.

Think about this. We are taught this by religion. We do and follow certain rules, and then when we die, we get our reward. We go to heaven? Wonderful, everyone wants to go to heaven. Let's not forget Adam and Eve were there. They had it made. Not only that, but come to think of it, Lucifer was also there. In Ezekiel 28:13, he was in Eden, the garden of God (Yahweh). Every precious stone was thy covering. In verse 14, he was the anointed cherub that covereth, God (Yahweh) has set him (thee) so.

> Thou wast upon the holy mountain of God (Yahweh), thou hast walked up and down the stones of fire. Thou wast perfect in thy ways from the day that thou wast created, till iniquity (lawlessness) was found in thee.

The point I'm making is: it didn't do any good to be there. If the lower aspects of mind or consciousness overwhelmed the higher or heavenly (God, Yahweh) mind or consciousness, you kick yourself out of heaven.

> The angel came down with the key to the bottomless pit with a great chain in his hand, and he laid hold on the dragon, that old serpent which is the devil, and Satan and bound him a thousand years. (Revelation 20:2)

The symbolism of this as an allegory is that when the one (which is God, Yahweh) with the zeros of eternity and divineness of God (Yahweh) that you get through meditation and prayer, when the spirit purges from the right side of the brain, and your eye is single, your whole body is full of light (Matthew 6:22). When this happens to you, the lower aspects of the mind are now controlled by the higher. Not that the lower mind won't try to come back. The thousand years mentioned here are not years at all. In 2 Peter 3:8, a day is as a thousand years. Time is not a factor. One is God (Yahweh) and a day in enlightenment.

Now twelve is the number of perfection by the Hebrew language. The twelve aspects of a year would be months as twelve months make a year. The twelve aspects of a day would be hours because twelve hours make a day. The twelve nerve centers of your body (perhaps even your chakras) and your mind, the twelve cranial nerves of your brain, six for each side, the right and left hemispheres. In Revelation 20:3, Satan was thrown in the bottomless pit, a seal was placed on him that he (Satan) would deceive the nations no more. In allegory, each person has two nations or countries within them. There is a high country and there is a low country. As in the Bible, there are the mountains and there's the valley, and also the desert is used. In Japan, the name of God is "Kami," which means "mountain town," and the name of the devil is "Shimo," which means "low lands."

When in Revelations it said about deceiving the nations no more, it is talking about an allegory the aspect of the human mind not being deceived anymore by thoughts or the lower mind. Almost every wrong is followed by "I just didn't know what I was thinking." Anyway, Satan is loosed for a little season after the thousand years and shall go out to deceive the nations which are in the four quarters of the earth.

In Numbers 2:2, it explains this in allegory. Judah is toward the east, Reuben is toward the south, Ephraim is to the west, Dan is to the north. Now as we have talked about, the spiritual part of your mind is from the east. The south represents the physical, and the west is the intellect, the north being the emotional aspect of the mind. The thoughts of the intellect (west) put out the spirit (east) light (spirit) of the divine (Yahweh). The west is where the sun sets brings the darkness upon the earth. Why is this created this way? The four corners of the world represent, in allegory, the emotions, spiritual, physical, and intellectual parts of your mind.

I will go back to the four stages of consciousness. China, starting from the lower to the highest, is as follows: earth, wood, metal, fire, water. In Greek, it's earth, water, air, fire, renewed mind. Now in German, it's earth, water, air, fire, light. When the Bible talks about deceiving the four corners of the earth, it is showing, as in all cultures, that earth is the first or lower stage of consciousness. It is referring to the natural or carnal mind. Your thoughts of doubts, worries, and fears all rise up from the emotions, which affect the rest of the aspects of your mind; the intellect, spirit, and even the physical is affected. Coming from the west or intellect, the spiritual insight or light is soon darkened. The light comes from the east or right side of the brain.

Now back to Revelation, in verse 8, Gog and Magog were gathered, whom as the sand of the sea, and in verse 9 of chapter 20; they went up on the breadth of the earth and surrounded the camp of the saints about and the beloved city, and fire came down from heaven and devoured them. Now Gog and Magog are modern-day Russia or northern countries or tribes. They came down from the north, which explained by allegory is the emotional aspects of the mind. They went up the breadth of the earth or lower mind or consciousness and compressed the camp of the saints about and the beloved city which is Jerusalem. Now in Galatians 4:26, "but Jerusalem which is above is free, which is the mother of us all."

Remember what we have talked about. In meditation, no thoughts or virgin consciousness, the child or (Christ) Yahshua (God), can be born in us, which is Luke 17:20—the kingdom of God (Yahweh) is within you. This mother (Jerusalem) is above (referring to your mind) the *dura mater* and the *pia mater*, which is the outer and innermost layers of the brain called the "hard mother" and the "tender mother." In Revelation 20:9, fire comes down and devoured them (Gog and Magog or emotional aspects of the mind), which is as unto a mother protecting her children. So the thoughts of the lower mind come back after meditation, but the fire of the spirit burns up or devours them.

This is spiritual, this is truth, this is allegory. This is hard to even understand, but the spirit teaches all things (John 15:26)

> But the comforter is come whom I will send
> unto you from the Father, even the spirit of truth
> which proceedeth from the Father, he shall testify
> of me. Me is the I am, that you are because you
> are God (Yahweh). (John 10:34)

> The kingdom is inside you. (Luke 17:20).

> Howbeit, when he the spirit of truth is
> come, he (it) will guide you into all truth. He (it)
> shall not speak of himself, but whatsoever he (it)
> shall hear, that shall he (it) speak, and he (it) will
> show you things to come. (John 16:13)

Now He is written because it refers to Christ being in you, and notice that the action part of that verse, where the Spirit is doing something, is written five times showing the five stages of consciousness (so this is done through meditation). This is how He (it) shows you or speaks to you.

> But the comforter, which is the Holy Ghost
> (spirit), whom the Father will send in my name
> (which we have talked about, means "in my
> way") this is meditation, being the way, he (it)
> will teach you all things and bring all things to
> your remembrance, whatsoever I have said unto
> you. (John 14:26)

So I can't teach you. No man can teach you, and no church (which is as we know or understand church to be, a teaching of religion) can teach you. Church, meaning the called-out ones, also means a body of believers, but it's also another name for the temple. The temple is made without hands, being on the sides of your head, being your mind. The "I am" that is in you is what teaches you all things. There is no end to the teaching of all things. Matthew 28:18–20 is what has been taught by most religions as the commission of the church. However, by allegory and spiritual understanding, it goes much deeper. It goes like this:

> And Jesus (Yahshua) came and spoke unto them saying all power is given unto me in heaven and earth, go ye therefore and teach all nations, baptizing them in the name of the Father, and the Son, and of the Holy Ghost (spirit); teaching them to observe all things whatsoever I have commanded you, and lo; I am with you always even unto the end of the world (age), amen.

Now what does it mean? In allegory, all power is given unto me. The me is the "I am" that you are because the kingdom of God (Yahweh) is within you (Luke 17:20). "In heaven and in earth" could be physical, but it's not. By the spirit—or, in allegory, heaven—refers to the higher mind or consciousness that's in you, and in earth is the lower or the first stage of consciousness or mind, ego, or human nature that's in us. Go and teach all nations as is shown back in Revelation 20:3 and verse 7, which we have gone over, is not nations at all but the four corners of the earth (the human mind) of the aspects of physical, intellectual, spirit, and emotions. Baptizing them, as we know, refers to water, being truth.

Now baptizing them in the Father's name would be the truth in Yahweh or God's way, which goes back to meditation. Of the Father and the Son and the Holy Ghost (spirit)—the three that bear witness, or the three attributes of God (Yahweh), being male, female, and both being the "El" or completeness of God (Yahweh). Teaching them to observe all things whatsoever I have commanded you—observing all things is another word for watching, and watching your thoughts is meditation. The I is the "I am" that is in you, that commands you. Lo, I am with you always even unto the end of the world. I am—that is, spirit that's in you that doesn't die—with you always, even unto the end of the age, which was at the end of the Pisces age. The truth is forever and will never leave you.

We have been taught and conditioned through religions on all matters, but on judgment and hellfire is another. The fact is that all knowledge is written down in one form or another, whether it's true or not. One thing is sure, it all comes out of someone's mind. So it comes from within. Many believe that if it's written down, then it must be true. It is that you go to church so they can teach you what they themselves believe that they themselves have written down. A point to note is that many congregations are not capable of thinking for themselves nor do their churches want them to. By religious means, you are either dumb or very dangerous or both. That is the problem with religion.

Remember in 2 Corinthians 3:6, "Who also hath made us able ministers of the New Testament; not of the letter but of the spirit, for the letter killeth but the spirit giveth life." In Revelation 20:11, "And I saw a great white throne and him that sat on it from whose face the earth and heaven fled away, and there was found no place for them, and I saw the dead small and great stand before God (Yahweh) and the books were opened and another book was opened which is the book of life and the dead were judged out of those things which were written in the books according to their works." Then verse 13, "And the sea gave up the dead which were in it, and death and the gave delivered up the dead which in them, and they were judged every man according to their works, and death and Hades were cast into the lake of fire, this is the second death and whosoever was not found written in the book of life was cast into the lake of fire."

Now if you took this literally or by the letter, this would be a judgment. The bad would be burned up and the good would be saved by their works. You were either written in the book of life or you weren't. Now there's one problem with all this, and scripture supports it. There's none good but one (Matthew 19:17). There's none righteous but one (Romans 3:10). God (Yahweh) is no respecter of persons (Romans 2:11; Acts 10:38; Colossians 3:25). I, the Lord (Yahweh), create good and evil (Isaiah 45:7).

In Romans 8:7, we have been over this. The carnal mind (your natural mind) is enmity against God (Yahweh). It hates God (Yahweh), said your Bible (not me), for it is not subject to the law of

God (Yahweh), neither indeed can be. I will say that again, neither indeed can be! It means it can't be. But how can you be judged on something you'll never be able to do in the first place?

Read what Jesus (Yahshua) says about this in John 5:24:

> Verily, verily, I say unto you. He that heareth my word and believeth on him that sent me hath everlasting life and shall not come into condemnation but is passed from death unto life. Now that means not coming into condemnation means not being judged.

Now hearing His words and believing in His words is doing what he said. He asked the question, "Why call me Lord, Lord (Master), and do not what I say?" (Luke 6:46). He said, "Seek first the kingdom of God (Yahweh) and his righteousness, and all these things shall be added to you (Matthew 6:33). The kingdom of God (Yahweh) is within you (Luke 17:20). So you put this together, the first thing you do is seek first the kingdom that is in you, and the only way of doing this is through meditation. So back to John 5:24, "Believing and doing you pass from death to life without judgment or condemnation." This happens before you die, not after. As it said, God (Yahweh) is not the God of the dead but of the living (Matthew 22:32; Mark 12:27; Luke 20:38).

Now if you compare those verses with the ones that say, "Now is the day of salvation. The kingdom of God (Yahweh) is at hand, believe the gospel," at hand means now. Now is now. These verses are 2 Corinthians 6:2 and Mark 1:15. This is spiritual, and passing from death to life is now, through meditation, that the virgin consciousness can be born in you. This is the allegory that's in Luke 21:29–32.

He spoke to them a parable (allegory): "Behold the fig tree and all the trees (now this *all* is really translated likewise or moreover)." This is a comparative, but he is really talking about the fig tree. Now let's go on. "When they now shoot forth, ye see and know of your own selves that summer is now nigh at hand."

And verse 31, "So likewise ye, when ye see these things come to pass, know ye that the Kingdom of God (Yahweh) is nigh at hand."

In verse 32, "Verily I say unto you, this generation shall not pass away till all be fulfilled."

Now there have been many generations that have passed away since then. So this is allegory, this is not literal. Some may say that it's referring to the generation that all these things are happening at the same time. They would be right. All these things could go back to verse 23: "distress in the land." Verse 25: "signs in the sun and moon (we have had the blood moons four fall the last couple of years on holy days [Jewish]—it would be the Feast of Tabernacles, Passover, Trumpets, Pentecost)."

Verse 28: "seeing the Son of Man coming in a cloud. Some we have seen, some we haven't."

Where the allegory comes in is in verse 29: "Behold the fig tree." Then it goes on: "When they now shoot forth" (this is other trees), the fig tree blooms from within (we have talked about this)."

You know summer is nigh at hand, and it said: "You see and know of your own selves." This is referring to meditation, the only way you truly see your own self. It is referring that you see and know of your own selves (know from within), and when the fig tree blooms (that's from within), "know it's nigh at hand" is right here (close).

Now in Luke 17:20, the kingdom of God (Yahweh) comes not with observation. It means you don't see it. Verse 28, "where the Son of Man coming in a cloud with power and glory," would seem to be a contradiction, but not when the air is the third stage of consciousness, and through your eye being single and your whole body being full of light (which is meditation), it all makes perfect sense.

Going back to Revelation 20:11, "This great white throne is your own consciousness, well, higher consciousness. Where it will convict you one way or the other. Now, the dead small and great is by allegory (you can be spiritually speaking about two types of the dead)." You can be dead spiritually, with no light or life, or you could be dead to the world, where you have turned from death unto life, where you are dead to the flesh and dead to the world, dead to the mind. Where you have killed the old man. This doesn't happen in the future, it happens now. When you let the spirit or fire from the right side of the brain to purge the left side of the brain through meditation, this is how you enter into life and is what is meant when Christ (Yahshua) said, "I am the way, the truth, and the life" (John 14:6).

I am is Yahweh, which means "I am that I am." We are gods (John 10:34). The kingdom of God is within you (Luke 17:20). Now the way is meditation, and taking no thought written five times in Matthew 6 shows the five stages of consciousness.

"The dead that stand before the throne or God (Yahweh) in Revelation 20:12, and the books were opened, and another book was opened, which is the book of life." Now in allegory or spiritually, you're looking at the human mind. The fact is, there are no such thing as dead people, only dead bodies. In 1 Corinthians 15:31, "I protest by your rejoicing which I have in Christ Jesus (Yahshua) I die daily."

Also in Daniel 8:11, "The daily is taken away; this is referring to meditation." The judgment of the dead is the reaction of your own mind to the decisions you have made in your life, to either be in the land of the living being within or to be in the land of the dead without. It's up to you. Let me explain. You are the temple of God (Yahweh). The kingdom of Yahweh is within you, so the throne of Yahweh or higher mind is as well inside you. This is allegory, this is spirit, this is truth. The truth shall set you free (John 8:32).

The true judgment goes against the things that hurt you. Not people, not things, but in a way, you. The God or higher consciousness frees you from the lower mind or death, the things you have been told or taught by the world, education, and yes, religion. It frees you through the books that were opened in Revelation 20:12. It's another book that was opened (the Book of Life). They were judged by the things written in that book by their works.

This Book of Life is described in Revelation 5:1:

> And I saw in the right hand of him that sat
> on the throne a book written within and on the
> backside sealed with seven seals.

This is written within, and the seven seals on the backside are the seven chakras which run up the spine and are referring to meditation in activating the pineal gland, opening the right side or spirit part of the mind, which is referred to as in the right hand of him that sat on the throne. The people that don't know about meditating or don't meditate have never read the book of life. They don't know about the Book of Life. They are the dead that are dead spiritually. I am speaking in allegory. Those that are alive are those that have killed the flesh or old man or carnal nature through the spirit or fire. The old man or carnal nature, our natural mind, is the 10 percent of all that we are, and in Matthew 22:37, Mark 12:30, Luke 10:27, Jesus (Yahshua) said, "You shall love the Lord thy God (Yahweh) with all thy heart, soul, and mind. So that's everything that you are."

So it's more than 10 percent? Not really. You only used 90 percent and is the blessings of heaven that will be poured down to you if you use the 10 percent. You see, this is the true meaning of tithing. This is the sacrifice, its true meaning. It's religions that started animal sacrifices and even human sacrifices. So by religion, the Lord came to bear witness to the truth, and through the cross set you free from sin by the law, and gave you life eternal, which is absolutely true if they really understood the allegories of what they were really saying. The truth of all things is through the spirit, which means the kingdom of God (Yahweh) is within you. The sacrifice (or death) represented by the cross is the way (we spoke of earlier) of meditation. This is where we die daily (1 Corinthians 15:31), and the ego or carnal mind is put to death. By no thoughts, there's no sin, and at that point, the mind can be purged by fire or spirit, which is what is meant by putting new wine in new bottles or wineskins. The virgin (virgin consciousness) or Christ can be born in you.

Religions have used baptism to represent this, but baptism (water) is only the first stage of consciousness, which starts the process, so it's very important, but you still have five stages of consciousness and seven chakras to go before the new mind, which is the Sabbath (rest), the six days of work and then the seventh, which is why it's holy. The six waterpots at the wedding were completely full until it was poured the seventh time to become wine. The number seven is all throughout the Bible. It's spiritual, it's allegory. If it was a doctrine, this would be what being born again would mean. Not of the flesh but of the spirit, if the spirit of God (Yahweh) is in you.

> If you have not the spirit of God (Yahweh),
> you're none of his. (Romans 8:9)

> Christ in you, the hope of glory. (Colossians
> 1:27)

We are physical, so we tend to think physically. We don't think within, which would be spiritual. Have you ever noticed most church stuff is outside? That's why we have temples and shrines and cathedrals and crosses, steeples, churches, preachers, etc. The temple without hands is on your shoulders (1 Corinthians 3:16–17); "Ye are the temple of ever learning all the time," said 2 Timothy 3:7, but never coming to the knowledge of the truth. Truth is not outward.

> Behold thou desirest truth in the inward
> parts and in the hidden part thou shalt make thee
> to know wisdom. (Psalm 51:6)

The hidden part is the inside. It's not seen and is hidden from our understanding.

> I will build my church and on this rock
> (Peter's name means little stone). (Matthew 16:18)

Most look at Peter as starting the church, but the fact is Christ is the Rock being spoken of (1 Corinthians 10:4), and that rock was Christ. What's interesting is the pineal gland is also called little stone. Like when David went to the brook and got five little stones and hit the giant in the forehead where the pineal gland is located. It was a brook because water was there as baptism or the first stage of consciousness; it was five stones showing the five stages of consciousness or the five senses. These are allegories, having deeper meanings.

Peter, church, Christ, pineal gland—it's all referring to the mediator between God (Yahweh) and man (2 Timothy 2:5). This Christ or the "I am" that's in you is Spirit, and the Spirit is life.

This word *Christ* is a Roman word. Constantine was called Christ, and it has been passed down from the Romans just as the word *Christians* was passed down. Christians were followers of Serapis long before Christianity was invented. The word *Jesus* was invented as well from Iesous in the Greek, from Iesus from the Romans, which we've talked about before. In the New Testament, the word *Christ* got translated from words like *Messiah, Savior, Master, chosen* or *anointed one*, or *Yahshua*. All these words come from the word *anointing* or *anointed one*. Kings were anointed with oil in ancient times. Oils are associated with wealth and royalty, and in religion, oil represents "spirit," which is a pouring out as water. Water also represents spirit and truth. In John 7:38, "Out of his belly shall flow rivers of living waters," and in Acts 2:17, "In the last days I will pour my spirit upon all flesh."

Christ (or the anointed one) and "Krishna" have the same meaning; chrism or claustrum is a fluid which through meditation from the solar plexus or belly flows upward to the pineal gland which opens up the right side of the brain. Christ can come on His white horse, which is the sixth chakra "Ajna" called the white horse.

> Behold I stand at the door and knock; if any
> man hears my voice and opens the door, I will
> come into him and sup with him, and he with
> me. (Revelation 3:20)

This door is of the mind between the two hemispheres of the brain. In Solomon's temple, there was a veil between the inner and outer courts, which was ripped in two when Jesus (Yahshua) died. This is allegory. No one could go into the holiest of holies or they would die. Once a year, the high priest went through washing and atonements and sacrifices and then was allowed in. The "I am the door of the sheep" in Revelation 3:20, what does that mean? Meditation. "If any man hears my voice and opens the door."

"My sheep hear my voice" and "the way to open the door" is the same as "he that hath the key of David, he that openeth and no man shutteth and shutteth and no man openeth." This is Revelation 3:7. This key that David had is meditation. In Luke 11:52, Jesus (Yahshua) said, "Woe unto you lawyers! For ye have taken away the key of knowledge: ye enter not into yourselves, and them that were entering in ye hindered." You open this door by meditation.

In 1 Corinthians 10:11, it said that "all these things happened for ensample: and they are written for our admonition upon whom the end of the world (age) are come."

So the stories of the Bible are there to teach us and show us spiritual lessons. That's where allegories come into play. In Revelation 19:10, "For the testimony of Jesus (Yahshua) is the spirit of prophecy." In 2 Peter 1:20, "No prophecy of the scriptures is of any private interpretation." So where prophecy (predictions) comes in, it's not any (self) understandings of it. It's not inside as spirit or allegory but plainly showed. I will show you what I mean.

When it said in 2 Timothy 3:1, "Know also in the last days perilous times shall come," you can look around and see this. In 2 Peter 3:3, "Knowing days scoffers walking after their own lust"—you can see that too. That's not an allegory. Isaiah 3:12: "That children are our oppressors and women rule over them." Now that is both allegory and true to life.

Our values are reversed in the family now. In allegory, our emotions (women) rule over our minds, and we are as children in our spiritual dealings with each other, which ends in this being our oppressors. "My children are destroyed for lack of knowledge" (Hosea 4:6). This can be both allegory and real life. Common sense is not common anymore. Yet we have all this knowledge and no wisdom.

In Daniel 12:4, many shall run to and fro, and knowledge shall be increased, and in verse 10, "many shall be purified and made white and tried; but the wicked shall do wickedly and none of the wicked shall understand, but the wise shall understand." We have mass transportation. To and fro is nothing anymore (worldwide). It was not so long ago. We have technology, communication, computers, Internet, science; and we have lust, greed, corruption, hate, and violence as well.

If we are so smart, then why do we still have these other things? Only the wise can understand. Yet the lack of knowledge (spiritual) that we can be purified and made white, that we have no character to control conduct, that there's no respect nor consideration of others, the knowledge to kill our nature, of overcoming our fears, lust, and wickedness, there is no understanding. The truth and purpose for being, of nature itself, of eternal life, this knowledge comes from within. It can only come from meditation. I can tell you, but you won't know it.

We have spiritual things all around us that we use every day and still don't know about it. How it really works. I have been blessed with music. Music is one of them. I can tell you everything about it, but if you are not blessed with it, you'll never learn it. It actually has allegories in its design just as we have been looking at in this book I'm writing. It has seven whole notes, eight if you count the octave. It has twelve if you count the half steps, sharps, and flats, and thirteen if you count the octave.

There are only twelve that make up millions and millions of songs that are all different throughout all history. Chords consist of thirds (major or minor if you flat the third or not). Major being a happy sound or minor as being sad or emotional, pretty, you could say. If you flat the third and the fifth, you have a diminished sound which is harsh and not that pleasing to hear. Now we've been over all these numbers before in the Bible and you can see them in music. How about the seven colors that are just in the rainbow by some chance that are combined to make up every color that's known? You have talents and gifts. Not everyone is an artist. Not everyone is mechanically inclined.

I have told you a lot about meditation. How it burns up the sacrifice or the carnal mind and gives spiritual understanding. This is what a living sacrifice is. This is what dying daily means. This is putting new wine into old bottles (wineskins). This is spiritual. The spirit has to kill the old nature in order that the new nature (the Bible said the new creature) can be born, which is born again. It said, "I make everything new."

You see it in nature, with the butterfly. The butterfly is a new creature. I don't know if you thought of this before. Once the caterpillar goes into its cocoon, it is no longer. How about lice and then flies? Even the seed of a plant. The seed provides the substances for the plant life. Once the plant has its own roots, the seed is not needed and dies. The plant will not live unless the seed dies.

That which thou sowest is not quickened
except it dies. (1 Corinthians 15:36)

There's a song used in most churches as an altar call entitled "Just As I Am." It's a moving song, and people would get emotional and would confess Jesus and give their hearts to the Lord and at that point become saved. Well, as sincere as that may be, using someone's emotions to bring about a lifetime commitment or judgment call can only instill in a person the (emotional) need or support of the church for his or her emotional needs, which in most cases would be a form of justification. They wouldn't know this, but it's almost a form of emotional bondage, a psychological control that churches have over people. This is not how God (Yahweh) works.

Second Corinthians 1:24 speaks that ministers, churches, etc. should not have dominion over your faith. Yet most do. Jeremiah 17:5 says, "Cursed is the man that trust in man."

Let God (Yahweh) be true, but every man a
liar. (Romans 3:4)

The Bible says different than what people and religions do. Superstitions, fear, and guilt are of the lower mind, which is lustful and evil. Churches promote the very things that they themselves speak against.

There was a movie out not so long ago called *Apocalypse Now*. It was about the end of the world. It had the doom and gloom and hopelessness of any end-times movie. What it does is promote more fear, stress, depression, which adds more to the consciousness of the lower mind. Seeing that we are gods (John 10:34), we are also creators, and this is only revealed by the spirit through the 90 percent of the mind that we don't use. Most don't understand because it is given through the spirit by meditation. So we are creators, and we create by consciousness.

The God (I am) Yahweh that's in us creates by consciousness. So to say this another way is that everything that is, is consciousness.

As a man thinketh, so is he. (Proverbs 23:7)

We create our own reality. This is how cause and effect works. This is how sowing and reaping works as well. This is how it's more blessed to give than to receive. This is why it's what's in a man that defiles him (Matthew 15:11). Even though it sounds like different things, it's all the same. We don't understand the nature of things, yet even looking at nature and studying it, you can soon see that it connects to each other; that is, its codependence of each other. One provides for the other's needs as the water cycles and food cycles, and the list goes on, proves. That is because everything is connected to this God (Yahweh), the universal consciousness. He's in one place and everywhere at the same time. In the beginning was the Word, the Word was God (Yahweh). We've talked about this, it's frequencies, the best we can define it. Everything is tuned to this. To whom can hear, let him hear. It's spiritual, yet as this age of Aquarius comes upon us, things are changing. It's changing in us and to us and all nature as well. These frequencies are speeding up. Spiritual forces that are way beyond our control are coming upon this world, and how we deal with these forces will be our test.

Now I'm not changing the subject, but if I told you hot and cold were the same thing, would you believe me? You know they are. It's temperature. It's just one is the extreme of the other. You got good and evil, they're both spirit. One is the extreme of the other. Religions would burn me to the stake by saying this, but it's true. These frequencies or spiritual forces will either be used to promote the higher mind or consciousness or the lower. This end-time or end of this age is revealed to us through the spirit. "Apocalypse" means the revealing, and so does the book of Revelation. It's warning us and is telling us about what is going on and what is going to happen in our mind. It's also showing us about "the way," meditation, which will cause us to connect to this consciousness.

"Apocalypse" is like the word *cult*. It has been falsely used by religions, I guess out of fear. One is used, meaning "revealing or revelation," and cult only means "hidden." Such words are used by religions to mean evil and to cause fear.

The four horses of the apocalypse (Revelation) don't mean anything like they are taught to mean. Horse means "knowledge or wisdom" in allegory as Paul was knocked off his horse or his understanding or his knowledge—the four understandings of revealing or revelations. These horses ride upon the earth (earth is the first stage of consciousness), and it is referring to the lower consciousness. Red symbolizes the emotions. I will get to this, but first Proverbs 4:6, to understand a proverb and the interpretation, the words of the wise and their dark sayings. Dark sayings mean more than what the words actually say, which is another word for allegory. As I have already said, we use them every day. Someone being three sheets in the wind, shooting your mouth off, or shooting the bull—they don't mean what the words say.

Now back to the four horses of the Apocalypse, which means the four understandings of the revealing or revelations. Now they are different colors. One is red, meaning the emotions. The other three are black, pale, and white. Red symbolically means the emotions. You see red when you get angry, for example. The devil is red. Santa Claus is in a red suit. The Red Sea. The red heifer. The emotions try to put you in bondage with the lower mind. This is ever getting stronger as the Aquarius age comes in. Watch the news as killings and fear grip our lives more and more.

The black horse or understanding is intellect. Why would intellect be black? The blackness of night blocks out the sun that rises from the east, which is spirit. West also symbolizes intellect. With your intellect, it will choke out the light of enlightenment every time. You can reason or think your way out of spiritual life and still not understand anything. Knowledge shall increase more and more, and it only leads to more wickedness.

Now, about the pale horse or understanding, it is the lowest mind, which is death. The pale horse is the effect of the other two: the out-of-control emotions and fear and the intellect trying to solve these issues, which it can't because it's all spiritual. Deep depression and hopelessness set in more and more, which destroys spirituality more than the other horses combined.

Then there's the white horse or understanding, which is spirit, and it is pure. In Revelation 19:11: "And I saw heaven open up and behold a white horse, and he that sat on him was called faithful and true, and in righteousness he does judge and make war."

This is the return of Christ (Yahshua), which is through the spirit. Remember the kingdom of God (Yahweh) comes not with observation (Luke 17:20). Starting with Revelation 6:2:

> And I saw, and behold, a white horse, and
> he that sat on him had a bow, and a crown was
> given him, and he went forth conquering and to
> conquer.

The bow is used to shoot upward or out from you as with meditation or your higher consciousness. Your mind is conquered as your thoughts are taken from you by the arrows and replaced with the mind of God (Yahweh). In Philippians 2:5: "Let this mind be in you that was in Christ Jesus (Yashua Messiah)," and by transforming your mind by renewing it is through study, proving it, and yes, most of all, meditation; that's in Romans 12:2. This is through the white horse or understanding. The crown is the seventh chakra, and it's called that.

The Sahasrara chakra, or seventh chakra, has the thousand petals or in Revelation 20:4, "lived and reigned with him a thousand years." Now along with the six chakras or Ajna, the white horse or hippocampus, Ammon's ram or ram's horn of your mind, which are the actual meanings of the words. These are parts of your brain. The *Stedman's Medical Dictionary* can prove this. The Ammon's Ram goes along with the Feast of Trumpets, being the first day of the seventh month.

You can also look at the five stages of consciousness. In Greek, lower mind, water, which is truth, the third that is no thoughts, the fourth which is fire, meaning spirit. The fifth is the new mind. Now the truth is religion is right with its symbols, the symbolism of baptism as water, and meeting Christ (Yahshua) in the air as rapture, which refers to meditation or no thoughts (an airhead), and that is where that saying comes from. Then it's the end of the world, that means age, and about fire coming down from heaven and burning up the earth, which the fire coming down is spirit burning up the earth or lower mind or consciousness, which is happening now at the Aquarius age. Now in Kabbalah, the five stages of consciousness are: action for earth, formation for water, creation for air, animation for spirit, and crown for the new mind, which is why the white horse of Revelation was given a crown.

In Revelation 6:3:

> And when he opened the second seal, I heard the second beast say, Come and see. And there went out another horse that was red, and power was given to him that sat thereon, to take peace from the earth, and that they should kill one another, and there was given to him a great sword.

The red is the emotions, which is the solar plexus or fire of the lower nature or mind. The emotional nature destroys us when passions and lust run out of control. The planet Mars is the red planet for war. The violence of the horse will be worse than ever in the Aquarius age.

In Revelation 6:5:

> And when he had opened the third seal, I heard the third beast say, Come and see. And I beheld, and lo, a black horse, and he that sat on him had a pair of balances in his hand. And I heard a voice in the midst of the four beasts say, A measure of wheat for a penny, and see thou hurt not the oil or the wine.

Now the black horse represents the intellect. The balances represent the weighing of decisions, which is through the carnal mind, not the higher mind. It is as weighing food by saying a measure of wheat for a penny. Religion reviews this as famine, and they're right, but in Amos 8:11:

> Behold, the days come, said the Lord God
> (Yahweh), that I will send a famine in the land,
> not a famine of bread nor a thirst for water, but
> of hearing the word of the Lord (Yahweh).

> He that has ears to hear, let him hear.
> (Matthew 11:15)

Wheat makes bread.

> Man doesn't live by bread alone but from
> every word that proceeds out of the mouth of
> God (Yahweh). (Matthew 4:4)

This hearing is understanding the Word of God (Yahweh). Now remember, intellect blocks out the sun or spirit from the east. The wine would be spirit, and the oil would be from the pineal gland from meditation. This is what is going on in the Aquarius age. The "hurt not the oil or the wine" is showing the way of surviving the age of Aquarius. In mysticism, wheat also means wisdom. A penny is like a mustard seed; it's a small amount, and the three measures of barley are love. In mysticism, barley means love. Three measures mean new life. Krishna, or chrism, claustrum, that comes up the spine through the seven chakras and impacts the pineal gland, bringing new life, or opening the window of heaven.

In Malachi 3:10:

> Bring all the tithes into the storehouse that
> there may be meat in my house.

Now in Revelation 6:7:

> When he opened the fourth seal, I heard the voice of the fourth beast say, Come and see. And I beheld a pale horse (understanding), and his name that sat on him was Death, and Hell followed with him. And power was given unto them over the fourth part of the earth, to kill with sword and with hunger and with death, and with the beasts of the earth.

The pale horse is the lower consciousness or the earth. You could say the physical aspect of man, which is death, our carnal nature or what we are. We can't be subject to the law of God (Romans 8:7). His name was death. Why? This is hard to understand and is different than anything you've ever heard before. Intellect never dies, emotions never die, and spirit never dies. The only thing that dies is the physical. Now the physical can kill the intellect or the emotions or the spiritual part of man. The carnal mind hates God (Yahweh). The horses of understanding have power over a fourth of the earth (the lower mind). The fourfold nature or attributes of man are physical, intellect, emotions, and spirit. Your nature resists this. Other people resist this. You'll be called crazy, a cult, and the religious people would be the first to throw stones.

One of Satan's names is *Cronus*, which means time. The physical will rob your time to meditate. God's (Yahweh) Word is as food. When Jesus (Yahshua) said, "Man doesn't live by bread alone," he meant it. Jesus (Yahshua) had to get off to himself to pray and meditate. You can starve yourself to death spiritually. We know the wages of sin is death (1 John 3:4). In Romans 8:7: "The carnal mind is not subject to the law of God (Yahweh), neither indeed can be."

Yet the more you kill the carnal mind and nature, the more you'll need the spirit not to do the works of the flesh. If you don't resist sin or you have power over sin and don't use it, you are in danger of killing yourself spiritually. You can sin against the Holy Spirit, which can't be forgiven.

> Wherefore I say unto you, all manner of sin and blasphemy shall be forgiven unto men, but the blasphemy against the Holy Ghost (spirit) shall not be forgiven unto men. (Matthew 12:31)

> For it is impossible for those who were once enlightened and have tasted of the heavenly gift and were made partakers of the Holy Ghost (spirit) and have tasted the good word of God (Yahweh) and the powers of the world to come, if they shall fall away, to renew them again unto repentance, seeing they crucify to themselves the Son of God (Yahweh) afresh and put him to an open shame. (Hebrews 6:4)

Yet this more than likely won't happen because you would have never been called in the first place.

> He which hath begun a good work in you will perform it until the day of Jesus Christ (Yahshua). (Philippians 1:6)

> For I am persuaded that neither death nor life nor angels nor principalities nor powers nor things present nor things to come nor height nor depth nor any other creature shall be able to separate us from the love of God (Yahweh) which is in Christ Jesus (Messiah Yahshua). (Roman 8:38)

These are all outside forces that can't separate you from the love of God (Yahweh), yet you can separate yourself from the inside, and the Bible tells you how.

There's a story in the Bible about Samson and Delilah. Now Samson was a Nazarite, "which no razor shall come on his head." His strength came from having long hair. Now he loved a woman in the valley named Delilah. At that time, the Philistines were over Israel. Israel had sinned or done evil in the sight of the Lord (Yahweh).

> And they were delivered into the hand of
> the Philistines for forty years. (Judges 13:1)

> And it came to pass afterward that he loved
> a woman in the valley of Sorek whose name was
> Delilah, and the masters of the Philistines came
> up unto her and said unto her, Entice him and
> see wherein his great strength lieth, and by what
> means we may prevail against him, that we may
> bind him to afflict him, and we will give thee
> everyone of us eleven hundred pieces of silver.
> (Judges 16:4–5)

As the story goes, Samson could have had a woman from his own nation, but he loved this Delilah. He did not see this woman as any threat to him. She kept asking him where his strength lieth. Samson said, "If you bind me with seven green withs that were never dried, then I'll be as any man." The Philistines were lying in wait.

Delilah said, "The Philistines be upon thee!" and Samson broke the withs as threads of tow are broken when it touches the fire. His strength was still not known to her. You would think this would have tipped Samson off to what was going on.

In Judges 16:11, again, Samson said to her, "If you bind me fast with new ropes that never were occupied, then shall I be weak and be as another man."

Delilah therefore took new ropes and bound him therewith, and said unto him, "The Philistines be upon thee!" And again they were waiting, and Samson broke the ropes.

In Judges 16:16: "And it came to pass, when she pressed daily with her words and urged him, so that his soul was vexed unto death, that he told her all his heart, and said unto her, There hath not come a razor upon mine head, for I have been a Nazarite unto Yahweh

(God) from my mother's womb. If I be shaven, then my strength will go from me, and I shall become weak and be like any other man."

Now the Philistines took him and put out his eyes and brought him down to Gaza and bound him with fetters of brass, and he did grind in the prison house. This is in Judges 16:21. Now after that, the lords of the Philistines gathered them together to offer a great sacrifice unto Dagon their god, in verse 23. Samson gets between the pillars upon which the house stood, he prays, God (Yahweh) gives his strength back to him one more time, and he pushed against the pillars and they fell, causing the building to fall, killing more Philistines at his own death than throughout his life.

Now, spiritually, what is this story about? What are the allegories? This is a man that can beat up a thousand men with a jawbone of an ass, kill a lion with his bare hands, and yet let this strange woman, that is not even of his nation, cut his hair and take away his strength. Not likely. There is something else about this story. This is mythology; this is a myth, which doesn't mean it's not true. This has great spiritual meaning. Samson means sun or light. The word *Delilah* means discouragement, languishment, and boredom. In other words, what can put the lights out? What you will find is that the higher mind or consciousness can be broken if it's going through a constant state of being discouraged by the lower mind. If the higher mind is constantly being exposed to discouragement from the emotions of the lower mind, you cut off the higher mind, especially if it's not being fed by the spirit through meditation.

Samson's strength comes from his long hair, and long hair pictures the upper growth of the higher mind or consciousness. Samson went to the valley to find this woman Delilah. "Valley" represents the lower mind, and "woman" means the emotions.

If you look at some of the acts he did before he got too involved with Delilah, you can find even more allegories. Samson kills a young lion. The "lion" refers to Leo the lion, which in allegory and the zodiac is represented by fire. It's the solar plexus or the Manipura chakra, which has the element of fire or ego. So Samson, through the spirit, is overcoming his nature. He kills a thousand with a jawbone of an ass (donkey), which represents the seventh chakra called

Sahasrara with a thousand petals. One with three zeros has great significance. One is for the oneness of God (Yahweh), and the zeros for the eternal of God (Yahweh). The three for the three attributes of Yahweh, as we have talked about, male, female, and both combined. The jawbone is the biting of the mouth or talking, the eating aspect of any animal, and is used as its defense or protection for most animals. It shows where the mouth can do great things either for your good or for your destruction.

A donkey (ass) is used showing the stubbornness of our nature. Here Samson is controlling the lower nature, using it even as a weapon to be used against his enemies. This is all symbolic to the aspect of man and his overcoming, which is only through the strength of his higher mind, which is through the spirit, which is the (hair) growth of one spiritually.

Now back to the story. Samson loved a woman in the valley of Sorek. Now if you look up Sorek, it means "choice vine." Now this is the best by looks, taste, and physical characteristics. This was not just any woman. The Philistines represent strangers, and in allegory would be the thoughts of the lower mind. These are the thoughts that come up from nowhere, out of the blue. These thoughts come from out of the world and from other people. They don't care about your thoughts at all, only that they line up with theirs. It's like religions; if you think other than the way they do, you become heathens, you are disfellowshipped or killed in the dark ages, destroyed. They want to prevail and overcome you, to bind you, to stop your thinking, speaking, or way. They want to enslave you. This is what the Philistines represent. They want to also afflict you and make you hurt and suffer. This is why bad things happen to good people. Now Israel was delivered into the hands of the Philistines for forty years. This represents the fourfold nature of man being physical, spiritual, emotional, and intellectual. Now the Philistines (strangers) and Delilah (discouragement) were working together.

Looking more closely at this, Delilah (discouragement) was more or less being controlled by the Philistines (the strangers). That's why the world by TV, music, sex, media, and the Internet——and the list goes on—all entertain the emotions; even religions do the same.

The gratification of emotional simulations through the senses or any physical means only leads to discouragement. That is why wants are never satisfied, and the world is so materialistic and greedy. These strangers use your emotions to control you for what they themselves want.

The masters of the Philistines were each going to give Delilah eleven hundred pieces of silver. Eleven hundred is interesting because it isn't twelve. Twelve is the number of perfection in Hebrew. Eleven doesn't quite make the grade. It may look good, it may sound good, and it may be close, but it's not twelve. Silver means the mind. That's why someone is considered wise having gray (or silver) hair. Now Samson kept playing around with the lower self. He said, "If you bind me with seven green withs that were never dried, I'll be as any man." Have you ever heard of a greenhorn or just being green? It means new.

They were never dried means that they were wet. Have you ever heard "you're all washed up" or "you're wet behind your ears"? Green and wet both refer to being new or inexperienced. How about the seven withs? Withs are small strings or vines used as ropes to tie. Seven are the seven chakras used in meditation (by being withs). It's small, so it's someone who hasn't been meditating long. It didn't matter because Samson broke them right away, as tow is broken when it touches the fire. Why fire? That is because fire is spirit. This is in context with the seven chakras and meditation, which we are talking about. The energy touches the pineal gland and opens the right side of the mind. That spirit can come over and purge the left side or burn in this case, killing the carnal mind.

This is why Samson moves the gate of the city up on a hill (Judges 16:3). The hill is the higher mind or consciousness, the city is the new Jerusalem, the kingdom of God (Yahweh) which is in you (Luke 17:20). The gate is the straight gate Jesus (Yahshua) talked about, which opens the left side of your brain (Matthew 7:13). It doesn't matter if you're new at meditation or not. Now the new ropes are the strong ones; it was seven of these as well. We make mistakes. We do wrong, but as long as there are seven chakras, prayers, and meditation and we use them, the fire or spirit burns or purges us, and there is nothing that can hurt or harm us. Delilah didn't stop. Every day, your lower mind is going to urge and entice you. The emotions of your lower mind—lust, greed, you name it. You are going to slip and fall, but when you give up, when you stop praying, and don't meditate, you stop going to the mountain and giving sacrifices, you stop the daily, and you stop watching, which are all metaphors or allegories of meditation.

Samson allowed his hair to be cut. He allowed the higher to be cut away. You can cut yourself off from God (Yahweh). No one else or nothing else can, but you can. Once this happens, the first thing to go is your sight or your insight. Your eyes are put out. You no longer understand what you once did. You don't want your wrong action or attitude to become a habit to the point that you don't even see or realize your wrong action. Now Samson was blinded and taken to Gaza and was bound with fetters of brass, and he ground in the prison, which is really where we are right now (prison). Wheat is what is ground, and wheat in mythology means wisdom or understanding. The world, as with religions, all grind. What they had at the time were giant wheels made from logs that prisoners were chained to, that spun around with a heavy disk that ground the wheat. They would walk around and around in a circle day in and day out and never go anywhere. That is the wisdom of this world (1 Corinthians 3:19).

> Ever learning and never able to come to the
> knowledge of the truth. (2 Timothy 3:7)

Now at the end of the story, Samson gave his life to destroy the Philistines (the strangers or thoughts of the lower mind). The lower mind would be as Scorpio, which is the betrayer as Judas by the emotional nature. This is astronomy. The third chakra is Manipura, which is not to be confused with Leo, the constellation of the Lion, but is the solar plexus and is where the fire or spirit starts gaining the force needed to burn the sacrifice in Aries the Ram. The Lion of Judah, which is the return of Christ (Yahshua) shown by the white horse or the sixth chakra, Ajna, of Revelation 6:2. Now the ram of Aries is to be sacrificed just as the lamb of God (Yahshua) for the world, which is symbolically you. You are to become a living sacrifice (spiritually) so you can have a virgin consciousness, which is represented by the constellation Virgo. This is when and only when Christ (Yahshua) can be born in you. You can't put new wine in old wineskins. The whole plan of salvation was written in the stars way before any paper.

Now what is salvation really? We have seen where Christ (Yahshua) told the Jews of his day, when he was about to be stoned, that "ye (you) are gods." The eternal consciousness that cannot die. Wonder if salvation is but a means of going home. A story in the Bible may address this very subject: the prodigal son, where there were two sons and the youngest wanted his inheritance, or as the Bible puts it in Luke 15:11–32, the youngest wanted his portion of goods that fell to him. He then left into a far country and wasted his substance with riotous living. Then a famine came, and he ended up feeding swine (pigs) and started eating the swine food. When he came to himself, in verse 17, he said, "How many hired servants of my father have bread enough and to spare, and I perish with hunger. I will arise and go to my father, and I will say unto him, Father, I have sinned against heaven and before thee, and am no more worthy to be called thy son; make me as one of your hired servants."

He went back to his father. His father saw him from afar and ran and fell on his neck and kissed him. His father gave him the best robe and put a ring on his hand and shoes on his feet. They got the fatted calf and killed it and had a party. "My son was dead and is alive again; he was lost but now is found."

Now the older son saw this and got mad and wouldn't go to the party. He told his father, "I've been with you the whole time, and you never had a party for me nor killed the fatted calf. This other son devoured thy living with harlots, and you have killed for him the fatted calf."

And his father said, "Son, you are with me always, and all that I have is yours. It is meet (it's the right thing to do) to be merry and glad, for your brother was dead and is alive again and was lost and is found."

There's a term that has been used called reincarnation, which many religions, mostly in the east, believe. Now the rest, to believe such a thing is not only wrong but many have been called cults for teaching such things, but these religions have nothing to do with anything even remotely related to this teaching. Now the word *reincarnation* is not in the Bible, it's true, but neither is trinity, rapture, Christmas, nor what is known as the apostle's creed or even the marriage ceremonies for that fact, which are read at weddings. Yet no one questions any of these teachings. It's other doctrines or customs taken from scriptures which have become whole religions or teachings that were never used or taught by Jesus (Yahshua) or the New Testament Church. One is "born again," the other one is talking in a mistranslation for little babies, confession, penance, and the list goes on, but are these what was actually taught? Most religions teach in general this: life is as a train track which leads to hell, but if you confess Jesus is Lord or get saved or baptized, the tracks will get switched, and then you would go to heaven, but not until after you die. Meanwhile, you have to go to church each Sunday, tithe 10 percent of your income, and believe everything they tell you. Well, in hell, you'll burn forever and ever, and if you go to heaven, you'll have to still be around these crazy religious people, so you more or less are done for either way. That's how I see it. The thing is, you have one shot to make it, and if you don't, it's time to be cooked. Fear is the factor used.

Now others, who know this is completely wrong, will tell you the world is deceived, that most of what is taught is wrong, that it's pagan in origins. They know hell only means grave. They know Saturday is really the Sabbath. They know about the true Holy Days (which, by the way, is where I was in my believing). I kept the Passover and cleaned my house of leaven. I kept the Feast of Tabernacles in the fall. I taught and knew I had the truth and was called, and I knew so much. Yet I wasn't tithing like I should have been doing, and I didn't call the leader of the church "that Prophet" and my family, and I have missed too many Sabbaths going to church. I was disfellowshipped and was told I wouldn't be going to the place of safety and that if I didn't repent, I would be going into the lake of fire. This is what religion has to offer you, and worse yet, this is what they teach God (Yahweh) has to offer you. One shot, or you're not.

What does the Bible have to say about reincarnation?

> If you will receive it, this is Elias, which was
> for to come. He that has ears to hear, let him
> hear. (Matthew 11:14)

Jesus (Yahshua) was talking about John the Baptist.

> All the prophets and the law prophesied
> until John, and if you will receive it, this is Elias,
> which was for to come.

It said this is Elias (it didn't say in the spirit of Elias as some churches say). It warns if you will receive it. I hope you receive it (understand it); most don't. You can just read over it. He that has ears to hear, let him hear. What does that mean? What kind of ears do you need to understand this stuff? Now let the Bible speak.

> To whom shall I speak and give warning, that
> they may hear? Behold their ears are uncircum-
> cised, and they cannot harken. Behold, the word
> of the LORD (Yahweh) is unto them a reproach;
> they have no delight in it. (Jeremiah 6:10)

Now being circumcised was a big thing and still is in some religions. If word of this gets out, there will be some group or another that will start circumcising ears.

> And his disciples asked him, saying, Why
> then say the scribes that Elias must come? And
> Jesus (Yahshua) answered and said unto them,
> Elias truly shall first come, and restore all things.
> But I say unto you, That Elias is come already,
> and they knew him not, but have done unto him
> whatsoever they listed. Likewise shall also the
> Son of man suffer of them. Then the disciples

understood that he spoke unto them of John the
Baptist. (Matthew 17:10)

Again, Jesus (Yahshua) said Elias is come. He didn't say in the
spirit of Elias.

If you want the real truth about now, Yahshua has come again.
The religions are looking for him on a white horse. Remember in
John 14:20: "In that day you shall know that I am in the Father,
and the Father is in me, and I am in you." Also in Luke 17:20: "The
Kingdom of God is within you."

Now you would think this verse would say differently. Let's see.

It's appointed for man once to die, and after
this the judgment. (Hebrews 9:27)

Yet in John 5:24, it reads, "Verily, verily, I say unto you; he that
hears my word, and believeth on him that sent me hath everlasting life, and shall not come into condemnation; but is passed from
death into life." It would seem that these verses would contradict
one another, but they are both true. You do have to die in order to
live. You can't put new wine in old bottles (wineskins). After this
comes the judgment. If you judge yourself, you shall not be judged
(1 Corinthians 11:31). You can die to yourself or you could die nat-
urally. The term "die in the Lord" is dying to yourself. We've talked
about killing the carnal nature through meditation by the spirit.

Now John 5:24: "He that hears my words (not everyone has
ears to hear; Matthew 11:14) and believeth on him that sent me
hath everlasting life." The "me" is the "I am" that's in you, the Christ
within, the hope of glory (Colossians 1:27), and "he" explains it better being Yahweh, the Father. I have tied these two verses together,
showing spiritually and in allegory the deep truths behind these
verses because if you took these verses literally, they would be contradictions. I will also show about "the prodigal son," how that ties
in and says about the same thing. We deal with what is known as
"karma." We make the cause and effects that touch us, good or bad.
We do this, not a devil, as religions will teach.

You are gods (John 10:34). You live eternally but decided to become physical. You made a choice and had help making it. Yet here you are in this pigpen of the carnal mind, and when you learn through the spirit, experience, and have had enough of the slop of this world that it has to offer, then what will come is the wisdom of the higher mind, and over many lifetimes, you will come to yourself (your true self) and you'll go back to the Father. In the prodigal son, the father said, "He was dead and is alive again." Do you want me to say that again? "Is alive again" means he was alive, died, and now is alive again.

This is an allegory. In the Bible, in the twenty-third Psalm, verse 4, "Yea though I walk through the valley of the shadow of death" (this is actually what we call life), you can't be again if you weren't before. He was lost but now he's found. The Day of Atonement pictures this "at-one-ment" with the Father (Yahweh), which was before. You were in your Father's house, but as any child, you leave your home to go out to learn.

Remember "go"? I'll hear it again. I know this is not easy to understand, but when you come to this understanding, which is only by the spirit (John 6:44), no man can come to me (me is the I am in you) except the Father which sent Me. Draw him, and I will raise him up at the last day.

The I or me is written three times showing the three attributes of God (Yahweh), and the last day refers to the Aquarius age. You die, but people don't die. There is no such thing as dead people. You only have dead bodies.

> And (I) say unto you my friends, be not
> afraid of them that kill the body and after that
> have no more that they can do. (Luke 12:4)

Then it goes on to say, "Fear him that is able to destroy both, spirit and body" in verse 5. It goes on to show your value: for the sparrows, being five are sold for two farthings and not one of them is forgotten before God (Elohim, Yahweh), even the very hairs on your head are numbered, fear not therefore ye are of more value than many sparrows. It does give a warning in verses 8–10:

> Whosoever shall confess (me) before men, him shall the Son of man confess before the angels of God (Elohim, Yahweh). He that denieth (me) before men shall be denied before the angels of God.

Verse 10:

> Whosoever shall speak a word against the Son of man, it shall be forgiven him, but unto him that blasphemeth against the Holy Spirit it shall not be forgiven.

Now it said if a word is spoken against the Son of man, it shall be forgiven. So the confessing of me and the denying of me in Luke 12:8–9 is not referring to Jesus (Yahshua), it's not the same me, because if you deny me before men, you shall be denied before the angels of God (Yahweh); this proves the allegory to be true. Now why would you be forgiven for speaking against the Son of Man and not for speaking against the "me" or Holy Spirit? For one thing, we have to come to that knowledge of "me," which we have said is only by the spirit. The Son of Man is interesting that no name is mentioned in this verse because the world doesn't even know his name. We have talked about that. Jesus, the name, where it comes from, and how we, not even knowingly, have been speaking against the Son of Man, but the "I am" that's inside—that's real power and revelation—that you're not going to receive until it's time for you to receive it. That you won't deny "me." That you really know who you are. That is the difference.

> I have yet many things to say unto you but you cannot bear them now. Howbeit, when the Spirit of truth is come, he (it) will guide you into all truth. It goes on to say, he (it) shall not speak

of his (its) own, but what he (it) hears that shall
he (it) speak. (John 16:12–13)

A very important verse in verse 14: "He (it) shall glorify 'me.'"
Has any religion told you about this? No, it can't. This "me" has
always been. This "I am." Where Christ (Yahshua) said, "You are
gods" (John 10:34), this doesn't die. Remember, only dead bodies.
When your car dies, and they do, you take it to the junkyard. You
don't stay there, do you? No, you get another car. A car is a temporary thing, and you are, as far as your body, that is. The Feast of
Tabernacles (the Jews' Feast) by the religions, even though they are
called Gods (Yahweh). Feasts in the Bible—why? Because they are
his temporary dwellings he stays in from lifetime to lifetime. This
is allegory. This is spirit. You make your temporary dwelling from
year to year. We have talked about this. This is not physical; this is
spiritual. In keeping the feast, you have temporary dwellings. Yet you
are a temporary dwelling physically. You are in a temporary dwelling
spiritually. That's why you must be born again. If you are not born
again spiritually, then you must be born again physically. This is why
it was explained to Nicodemus: "That which is flesh is flesh and that
which is spirit is spirit. Marvel not that I said unto thee ye must be
born again. The wind bloweth where it listeth, and thou hearest the
sound thereof, but canst not tell whence it cometh, and whither it
goeth; so is everyone that is born of the spirit."

Nicodemus said, "How can these things be?" He didn't know
then and they don't understand now.

> What man knoweth the things of a man save
> the spirit of man which is in him? Even so, the
> things of God (Yahweh) knoweth no man, but
> the Spirit of God (Yahweh). (1 Corinthians 2:11)

The Spirit of God (Yahweh) knoweth no man except the Spirit
of God, so this spirit of man has to be also the Spirit of God (Yahweh)
to a lesser degree for sure, in order to even understand the things of
God (Yahweh). So you are in a temporary dwelling. You come back

again in the womb of another human mother. You have different parents, different training. Your memories are stored in the 90 percent that you don't use. Then you start your tithing again on the 10 percent that you use. How long it takes for you to become what you need to become doesn't matter because time doesn't exist. You can be put back in time or ahead in time, depending on your training.

In dreams, have you ever met someone that you know in the dream but have never met before? You may have been to places you have never been before, but you know where you are. You may have been doing something and this strange feeling comes over you that you have done this before. This all comes from past life experiences. You see, death is but the end of a chapter, but it's not the end of the story. You can see where the evil prosper and have abundance, and they may have this their whole lives, but they can't take it with them, and you can surely know that they will have need and know what their evil deeds do, once it's done on them in the next life.

You will learn from your mistakes one way or another. God (Yahweh) is no respecter of persons (Romans 2:11; Acts 10:38; Colossians 3:25). It is written three times in the Bible, showing the three attributes of God (Yahweh). It doesn't matter how many chapters you have been through because when the story is over, you win. At the start of this, I said to remember the words *go out* that you would be hearing them again.

> He that overcometh shall I make a pillar in
> the temple of my God (Yahweh), and he shall go
> no more out, or go out no more. (Revelation 3:12)

It is believed that sin can be passed down from one generation to another. It is sure you learn your wrong from your parents that can be passed on, but it is the person himself that is doing the sin. This is gotten from Exodus 20:5, visiting the iniquity of the third and fourth generations. Now if you look in Ezekiel 18:20, "a soul that sinneth, it shall die; the son shall not bear the iniquity of the father, neither shall the father bear the iniquity of the son." In John 9:2, his disciples asked him, saying, "Master, who did sin, this man or his parents, that he was born blind?" Now most religions look over this question. Now if this man was born blind, how could he have sinned? The only answer that it can be is this man had lived before.

The most important part of you is not you. They can open you up and not see your thoughts, desires, dreams, and hopes, or feelings, or fears, but they're there. You are there, too, and you'll always be because you're not physical (not the real you). In Genesis 1:26, "Let us (Elohim) make man in our own image, after our likeness." The likeness part has made people see God (Yahweh) just as we are. In looks maybe, but God (Yahweh) is spirit (John 4:24). In Numbers 23:19, it said plainly, "God (Yahweh) is not a man.: So the real image or the real you is spirit.

In Matthew 16:13, Jesus (Yahshua) asked Peter, "Who do men say that I am?" Peter replied, "Some say that you are John the Baptist, some say you are Elijah, others say you are Jeremiah, and others say you are one of the prophets."

What is strange about this is that all of these people are all dead. Why would people be saying that he's one of these people in the first place? The fact is reincarnation was a common belief at that time. Jesus (Yahshua) never questions what they ask. If that concept was wrong, wouldn't you think he would be on top of all it? Jesus (Yahshua) did not put down the thought of reincarnation as one being spirit coming back in someone else as someone else.

We are conditioned in our minds by our environment. Thereby, we are taught directly or indirectly by the conditions we are subject to: parents, education, religion, work, and government. We take as truths what we are told or taught by and which we have respect for. Emotions and feelings become our means that become our conflicts. It's hard to see past our convictions and pride, to find out and know that what you have believed and lived by for all of your life are nothing but lies. To simply start killing all your insights and very life, which is what's meant by taking up your cross and following Matthew 16:24 and Mark 8:34.

What is the truth about the resurrection? There is a resurrection, but there are assumptions about it, that you are brought back as you are now. In 1 Corinthians 15:42, so also is the resurrection of the dead. It is sown in corruption, it is raised in incorruption. And in verse 44, it is sown a natural body, it is raised a spiritual body. Now in verse 50, this I say, brethren, that flesh and blood cannot inherit the kingdom of God (Yahweh). Now if you compare that with John 3:6, that which is born of the flesh is flesh, and that which is born of the spirit is spirit. Then in verse 8, "The wind bloweth where it listeth, and thou hearest the sound thereof but canst not tell whence it cometh and whither it goeth; so is everyone that is born of the spirit."

How come you can't tell? Because you can't see it. It's spirit. Like it said, so is everyone that is born of the spirit. Do you know being born of the spirit and being resurrected is the same thing? Corruption doesn't inherit incorruption.

In 1 Corinthians 15:36, "You fool"—pretty strong words— "that which thou sowest is not quickened except it die." When you plant a seed in the ground, that becomes what feeds the plant that grows. Then the plant has its own roots and can provide for itself. The seed dies for the plant to live. The flesh dies. I'm not saying the resurrection didn't happen. I'm saying religions don't explain it. Being born of the spirit is not going around telling people you must be born again and saying that you are born again. If you are still flesh and blood, you can't be born again. It's only written one time in the Bible where Christ (Yahshua) tells this religious leader something that he should have known.

He said unto him, "Art thou a master of
Israel, and knowest not these things?" (John 3:10)

What I have written in this book would not be known to most traditional religions. It's mysticism, mythology, astronomy, and above all, spiritual understandings. It's something else, which I have touched a little about, and that's psychiatry, which deals with the mind. The twelve we have talked about being the Hebrew number of perfection is also the twelve signs of the zodiac, the twelve months of a year, and the twelve hours of a day. It's also the twelve tribes of Israel and the twelve disciples. Zodiac doesn't come from the word *zoo* as many believe but from the word *zoo-o* (the last "O" being the long O sound). It means "the way," which refers to the seven chakras and meditation. Hippocrates, the Greek physicist and physician, said a doctor that doesn't have a full understanding of astronomy has no right to call himself a doctor. So this twelve of the zodiac and astronomy, the universe, the Bible, and even the human body, which consists of twelve systems: the skeletal system, muscular system, cardiovascular system, lymphatic and the immune systems, respiratory system, digestive system, endocrine system, urinary system, reproductive system, nervous system, and the integument system.

Now the mind and the body are all connected. Another interesting thing is the human mind has twelve cranial nerves, which surround the tabernacle or the temple that is in the center of the human brain. They are called as follows: olfactory, optic, motor oculi, trochlear, abducent, facial, trifacial, auditory, glossopharyngeal, pneumogastric or vagus, spinal accessory, hypoglossal. The cosmos to constellations, to the Bible, to now the brain. In 1 Corinthians 3:16, you are the temple of God (Yahweh), for the temple of God (Yahweh) is holy, the temple you are (Acts 7:48). The Most High dwells not in temples made with hands (Galatians 4:26), but Jerusalem which is above is free, which is the mother of us all.

The *Stedman's Medical Dictionary* gives a description of the construction of the human brain. The twelve cranial nerves connect at the *dura mater*, which is the outermost layer of the brain. A tough covering that anchors the brain, *dura mater* means "hard mother." The innermost layer is called the *pia mater* or "tender mother." There's a thin, delicate membrane called the arachnoid, which is also called the web, veil, or curtain. Just as the temple is described in the Bible as having an inner and outer court, with a veil separating both of them (Exodus 39:34, 30:6). It's a reticulated layer of tissue that resembles a spider web.

The hippocampus of the brain is the place of memory. There's an organ called Ammon's horn, used as the ram's horn or shofar in the Bible. The sixth chakra, or Ajna or pineal gland of the brain. In the brain, the *stria pinealis* connects the fornix with the pineal gland.

> Straight is the gate and narrow is the way,
> which leadeth into life, few be that find it.
> (Matthew 7:14)

In meditation, the energy coming up the spine and hitting the pineal gland travels the *stria pinealis* (straight gate) and ignites the fornix. In Daniel, the fiery furnace represents the fornix, which after the fire was heated up seven times more, the three—Shadrach, Meshach, and Abednego—which in allegory are the three of the fourfold natures of man being physical, mental, and emotional, and then the spiritual saves all three. The seven being the seven chakras that the oil or spirit is heated up by doing meditation.

Now looking at the cosmos, Pegasus, the constellation, by the myth, whose father was Poseidon being of the sea, was the white seahorse. The hippocampus of the brain also means white seahorse. This is the white horse of Revelation. Leo, the lion, would be the sign of fire for the pineal gland that in ancient times was called the pine cone. The pine cone explodes when hit by fire and is used for starting fires.

Interestingly, on June 10, 1998, the *Associated Press* reported from San Diego that astronomers for the first time had cracked a curtain of interstellar dust known as the Zone of Avoidance that blocks earth's view of a fourth of the universe. The supernova (eye in the sky) is in position as is the constellation Fornax (the furnace). This fire is flowing as this new age (Aquarius) comes in. This is going to change the earth's magnetic fields, causing great changes upon the earth, and also in the minds of men.

The book of Revelation reveals this happening. The fire coming down is spiritual energy. That is what the sevens are all about throughout Revelations. The seventh angel or angel of light will be as a frequency. Those whose polarization is scattered will have a difficult time, but for those who are flowing in a plane of harmony through meditation into polarization will rise above all the confusion, and a change in consciousness will be the result. So allow your pineal gland to polarize with the light for you and all of your house.

We have learned from the Bible in Galatians 4:24 that it is written in allegories. We have also been shown that the scriptures are not of the letter but of the spirit. In 2 Corinthians 3:6, "the letter killeth, but the spirit giveth life."

Now, to prove this, I will show scriptures that if they were taken literally would cause a lot of confusion, and it would also bring nothing but contradictions to the Bible.

> Then went up Moses and Aaron, Nadab, and Abihu, and seventy of the elders of Israel, and they saw the Elohim of Israel and there was under his feet as if it were a paved work of a sapphire stone, and as it were the body of heaven in his clearness. And upon the nobles of the children of Israel, he laid not his hand; also, they saw Elohim and did eat and drink. (Exodus 24:9–11)

> Not that any man hath seen the Father, save he that is of God (Yahweh), he hath seen the Father. (John 6:46)

> No man hath seen God (Yahweh) at any time. (1 John 4:12)

> And Jacob called the name of the place after the pineal gland (Peniel), for I have seen God (Yahweh) face to face. (Genesis 32:30)

This is where Jacob wrestles a man (Yahweh). You can't see God (Yahweh) with two eyes, but you can with one, the pineal gland, through meditation by the spirit. So this is not a contradiction. Genesis 17:10–15 is a covenant made between God (Yahweh) and his people forever, that every male child shall be circumcised or be cut off from his people. This is an everlasting covenant by God (Yahweh) forever.

> Behold I Paul say unto you, that if ye be circumcised Jesus (Messiah, Yahshua) shall profit you nothing. (Galatians 5:2)

It's an allegory. The male is the mind, where the outer desires must be cut away. This is spiritual.

> To whom shall I speak, and give warning, that they may hear? Behold, their ear is uncircumcised, and they cannot hearken: behold, the word of God (Yahweh) is unto them a reproach; they have no delight in it. (Jeremiah 6:10)

I guess if we went by this, we would be cutting one another's ears.

> Then spake Solomon, God (Yahweh) said that he would dwell in the thick darkness. (1 Kings 8:12)

> Talking about God and his son (Yahweh and Yahshua), who only have immortality, dwelling in the light. (1 Timothy 6:16)

Now we know the darkness is meditation, but if you took this literally, you would be in trouble.

How about Matthew 19:26, where it said, "With God, all things are possible"?

> And God (Yahweh) was with Judah; he drove out the inhabitants of the mountain; but he could not drive out the inhabitants of the valley, because they had chariots of iron. (Judges 1:19)

So maybe God (Yahweh) can't do everything. Chariots of iron are just too much for Him to deal with. Why is this in the Bible? Explain this! Iron in mysticism means "mental power." When they were building the temple in 1 Kings 6:7, there was no sound of hammer nor axe nor tool of iron heard in the house. This is an allegory about meditation, of no thoughts, which would be no mental power.

The chariots were in the valley, which is the lower mind or the carnal mind, the lower consciousness. So there's no contradiction.

Here is another one.

> Marvel not at this, for the hour is coming in which all that are in the graves shall hear his voice, and shall come forth: they that have done good unto the resurrection of life and they that have done evil unto the resurrection of judgment. (John 5:28)

> As the cloud is consumed and vanisheth away; so he that goeth down to the grave shall come up no more. (Job 7:9)

So it seems the Bible can't make up its mind. Which one is it? Are you resurrected or do you just die? We have talked about this, which the world doesn't understand. You are in a temporary dwelling, and your body doesn't come back anymore. The resurrection of judgment is not a sentence but a period of time. For if you remember in John 10:34, Jesus (Yahshua) said, "Ye (you) are Gods," but the only you that can be is spirit, for God (Yahweh) is spirit (John 4:24). The death of the body is not the death of you. Not if ye (you) are God (Yahweh) as Jesus (Yahshua) said.

Now in Mark 1, Jesus (Yahshua) was baptized by John the Baptist and, in verse 12, immediately after he was baptized, "The spirit driveth him into the wilderness for forty days to be tempted of the devil."

According to John 1, after he was baptized, two disciples followed him. One was Andrew, and they met up with Simon and Philip. And in verse 2, the third day, there was a marriage in Cana, and Jesus (Yahshua) and his disciples were there, and that is where water was made into wine. Now the question is, how could He be in two places at the same time? The forty days or enlightenment are the fourfold nature of man, being physical, mental, emotional, and spiritual. The zero shows the eternal significance of the four. The wilderness is meditation.

Jesus (Yahshua) just went into meditation. Now this shows that you can't go to the marriage until you go into meditation or go into the wilderness. So this is spiritual.

> If I bear witness of myself, my witness is not true. (John 5:31)

> Though I bear record of myself, yet my record is true. (John 8:14)

Now go back to John 5, back to verse 30, which said, "I can of mine own self do nothing." Now in Matthew 28:18, "All power is given unto me in heaven and in earth." It would seem to be a direct contradiction. Yet the I am that is God (Yahweh) is me, and you could say this about yourself. That all power is given unto me in heaven and in earth. If you know the me that is within you.

> If one smite thee on thy right cheek, turn to him the other... To love your enemies, bless them that curse you. (Matthew 5:39, 44)

This is what Jesus (Yahshua) taught. Yet this is the same man in John 2:15 who made a scourge of small cords and drove out the money changers and overthrew the tables. This is driving out the thoughts of your mind (the temple without hands). He also said in Luke 14:26, "If any man hate not his father and mother, sister and brother, and his own life, he cannot be my disciple."

> Love not the world nor the things that are in the world, and it goes on to say, or the love of the father is not in him. (1 John 2:15)

Yet in John 3:16, "For God (Yahweh) so loved the world that He gave his own begotten son, that whosoever believeth in him should not perish but have everlasting life." So, clearly, He (Yahweh) doesn't follow His own teachings.

Now the disciples were not even sure when Jesus (Yahshua) died.

> Now the first day of the feast of unleavened bread was when they had the last supper, where Jesus was betrayed that night by Judas.
> I will let you know that Passover is on the fourteenth of Abib and then the fifteenth to the twenty-first, the days of unleavened bread. (Matthew 26:1, 47)

Now John said in John 19:14 that it was the preparation of the Passover when Jesus (Yahshua) was being crucified, which would have been on Abib, which would have been a day before they had their first day of unleavened meal, and which would have been after he was already put on the cross.

A lot of things don't add up if you took the Bible literally. In Matthew 28:1, there were two women going to the sepulchre. In Mark 1, there are three women. In Luke 24:10, it's at least five women. In John 20:1, there is only one.

Now looking at the numbers in mysticism, one is the oneness of God (Yahweh), two is the duality of God (Yahweh) in that everything created has a duality. Three is the completeness of God (Yahweh) being the three attributes of God we talked about (male, female, and the both combined). The five women that were wise and had oil for their lamps, I think, refer to the five stages of consciousness, being earth, water, fire, air, and the divine mind, but it can also refer to the five senses: touch, taste, hearing, smelling, sight.

Another thing was the ascension when Jesus (Yahshua) goes back to heaven. In Matthew 28:16, they were to meet in Galilee, and in Luke 24:33, they were to meet in Jerusalem, and he led them out as far as Bethany, and He blessed them and was carried up into heaven (vv. 50 and 51). Sounds wonderful except Jerusalem is about one hundred miles from Galilee, and the book of John never mentions the ascension. It was the transfiguration where in Matthew 17:2, where Jesus takes Peter, James, and John to this high mountain and is transfigured in front of them and shone as the sun. They meet

Moses, Elijah, and a bright cloud comes over them, saying, "This is my son, hear him." This is one of the greatest events in the universe, recorded also in Mark 9:2. In both cases, John is there. Yet John never mentions it. It is not found anywhere in the book of John.

The point of showing some of these contradictions, which there are many, many more, is not a matter of the Bible being right or wrong. The truth is shown not in the words as they are shown in the spirit. It's a spiritual book, not a history book, not a storybook, even though it has stories in it as well as history. Understanding what the Bible is saying to us in its symbols and occult terms (occult means hidden). We've learned the many allegories, but how many more are there that the Bible holds?

In Revelation 4:1, it talks about a door opening. In Revelation 10:2, there's a small book mentioned. Both these verses have the same allegories in them. Let's take a look at them.

> After this I looked, and behold, a door was opened in heaven, and the first voice which I heard was as it were of a trumpet talking with me, which said, "Come up hither, and I will shew thee things which must be hereafter." (Revelation 4:1)

What things did this trumpet show? In verse 2, it was a throne in heaven with one sat on it. Verse 3 shows how the man looked, as a jasper and sardine stone, and a rainbow was round about the throne which looked as emerald. Verse 4: "There were twenty-four seats and elders sitting in them. They were dressed in white with crowns of gold."

Verse 5: "Lightnings and thunderings and voices proceeded out of one of the throne, and there were seven lamps of fire burning before the throne, which are the seven spirits of God (Yahweh)."

It goes on, but we will stop there.

Now in Revelation 10:2, let's see what that has to say. Verse 2, "And he had in his hand a little book open, and he set his right foot upon the sea, and his left foot on the earth."

In verse 3, "This angel with the book cried with a loud voice as a lion roareth, and seven thunders uttered their voices."

Verse 4, "Now when this happens (I was about to write), a voice from heaven said not to write, but to seal up the things the seven thunders uttered and write them not. Now in verse seven: In the days of the voice of the seventh angel, when he shall begin to sound, the mystery of God (Yahweh) should be finished, as he hath declared to his servants the prophets."

The book was eaten in verse 9, and in verse 11, "He said to me, 'Thou must prophesy again before many people and nations and tongues and kings.'"

Now what does this mean? In Revelation 4, a door was opened in heaven. In Revelation 10, a book was opened by an angel, which had his right foot on the sea, and his left foot upon the earth. We know by allegory that sea or water is truth and the right side refers to the right side of the mind or heaven, and the earth is the first stage of consciousness or the lower mind, being man. Being opened means being revealed to understanding. The door is the veil of the temple between the left and right hemispheres of the brain, which is opened through meditation. So both of these verses are saying the same thing.

In Revelation 4, a trumpet is a voice which says come up hither, which is the sixth chakra Ajna or the white horse, and Ammon's Horn, which is an Egyptian deity whose symbol is a ram. We have talked about the ram's horn or shofar blown on the Day of Atonement. This is also the pineal gland or the hippocampus of the brain. This coming up is the meditation, and the trumpet is the Ammon's Horn.

Back to Revelation 4, there was one on the throne, a wonderful sight, but there were twenty-four seats and elders in those seats dressed in white and golden crowns on them. They were dressed in white because they were pure and have overcome the fourfold nature of man, which is what the twenty-four is all about. The reason it was twenty-four was that the two in front of the four shows the duality of the four. The physical, mental, emotional, and the spiritual all can be either used by the higher mind or the lower mind. Also as male and female, the mind and intellect being male, and the female being the emotions and spirit. We've talked about this before. They were given crowns of gold for their overcoming. Now keep this in mind that this is in the mind and is spiritual.

Now in Revelation 10, the angel cries with a loud voice as a lion; this could be as a trumpet. We know "lion" is for Leo and is a fire sign. As the ram is burnt by the fire in meditation, the seven thunders utter their voice, where in Revelation 4, there were lightnings and thunders coming out of one of the thrones. We know this is talking about the seven chakras, for once the energy or fire hits the sixth chakra or pineal gland (pine cone), the right side or spirit burns up the sacrifice (the ram).

The seven lamps are burning before the throne, which are the seven spirits of God (Yahweh), which is the Book of Life of Revelation 5 or the seven chakras. Now this was to be written down but was told by the angel not to write. In Revelation 10:4, the things the seventh thunders uttered are to be sealed up.

In verse 7, "But in the days of the voice of the seventh angel before it sounded, a voice, in verse eight, said to take the little book out of the angel's hand, and to eat it."

Now in Revelation 10:9, "The little book was eaten, and in his mouth was sweet as honey, but in his belly was bitter." It's funny, but in Proverbs, the pineal gland is referred to as the honeycomb. Now in the days of the seventh angel was when the little book is revealed, that's why the book was eaten. After that, in verse 11, "Thou must prophesy again before many people, nations, and tongues."

The days of the seventh angel is the Aquarius age, that meditation through the seven chakras, which is our ark, to go inside ourselves, which is the seal placed on the foreheads in Revelation 7:3, 9:4, 14:1, 22:4.

Now there is an evil mark, being the mark of a man, that we have talked about in Revelation 13:16 and 20:1. This may be the little book that I am finishing up now. Have you heard anything like this before? Well, it is being revealed more and more as this age comes in. The book being opened from its seal or the opening of a door. This is our window of opportunity. We have looked at quantum theory and physics at the molecular level. We have seen how photons can think. This has been hidden from us all our lives. That there is a mind, a consciousness in the universe, that the universe actually thinks.

Physics has proven that light thinks. It's the trumpet, which is the ohm that is the center of the universe and is the center of our being. It's also a term for measure resistance, as an electrical term. The energy in meditation going through the resistance of the chakras up the spine, the throne of Revelation 4 as being the higher consciousness. We've talked about spirit and emotions, how they have to be in harmony with each other.

In the many allegories, the Bible teaches about these two aspects of being. We know that no amount of study or knowledge can help you nor churches nor any baptism nor religious means unless you can touch through meditation that you can be changed through the spirit or fire. You must understand things above religions. For all our lives, we have been to churches, never knowing the self nor the nature of God (Yahweh) or Spirit, which has been revealed in this book. Nature itself thinks and is a part of this, that we are all connected one to another, and that there are no spaces in between. Your consciousness makes electrons move and atoms and protons and all matter. That's what *I am* does and that's what *I am* is and what *I am* means. That is what our purpose to become is. We've learned through history why and what religion is and how it has changed and developed our consciousness to our reality we live in now, the lies told and taught, which is through deception, guilt, and fears that have produced the madness, violence, and hate we live in each day. We learned that we are Gods (Yahweh) in John 10:34. We can change this through and by consciousness if we become one, which can only be done by the Spirit.

We've learned this by the Bible, science, and seen by astronomy and by psychiatry, mysticism, and mythology the same universal truths. We've learned about the physical makeup of the brain with the energy centers of the chakras with the use of meditation. We have the symbolical meanings of the scriptures, the allegories, and their meanings, the different beliefs of different religions. Spiritual meanings of many different subjects along with history, which what anyone believes, even myself, if it doesn't work, then it isn't true. There are many that think I'm crazy. That's fine, I wonder myself sometimes. All I ask is that you search and check out this stuff for yourself. Then you can either know that I'm crazy or you can find out that there might be something to what I have said. Anyway, you will be better for it.

The number 7 is found throughout the Bible. It is truly holy. It has the fourfold nature of man: physical, emotional, intellect, and spirit. It also has the three aspects of God (Yahweh): male for mind and intellect, female for emotion and spirit, and then the "el" for God (Elohim), which would be the mind + spirit = God (Yahweh), and then you take the four, then add the three, you have the seven, and "The Seventh That I Am," the true purpose for which we are. That's why I named this book *The Seventh That I Am*. I know that I've finished this writing of the little book as a prophecy for many people, nations, and tongues and have done this not of myself but by the *I am* that's in us all, the children of light forever, that all shall be all in us and made known to us and by us all. That's all.

About the Author

Terry Clark grew up in Westmoreland County, Virginia, subjugated by being boss-eyed and introverted, and used music as a getaway. He found deep reflection in searching for truth and enlightenment to find hope, clarity, and inner peace. He now wants to share his findings to help the masses in their search for freedom and inner peace.